Poetic Potpourri

Maxine Spyres Hixon

Maxine Spyres Hixon

FIRST EDITION

All rights reserved, including the right of reproduction in whole or in part in any form.

Copyright @ 2007 by Tena M. Hixon and Pamela Hixon Rhea
Published 2010

Published by Brentwood Christian Press
Columbus, Georgia 31904

Printed in the United States of America
Library of Congress Catalog Card No.: TXu 1-593-346

10-Digit ISBN – 1-59581-540-6
13-Digit ISBN – 978-1-59581-540-8

Dedication

For Tena, Pamela, Ronald and Rodney, who were taught to quote John 3:16 when they first began to talk. All were saved at an early age, and were passed the torch to "carry on" in the service of the Lord, until God calls their name.

Biography

Maxine Spyres was born on January 29, 1926, in Adair County, Stilwell, Oklahoma. She married Carl W. Hixon on October 6, 1945 in Selma, California. They have four children: Tena, Pamela, Ronald and Rodney.

Maxine attended the Northeastern State Teacher's College in Tahlequah, Oklahoma. She taught school during World War II in a one-room schoolhouse — children of all ages.

Maxine's collections of inspirational poetry recently published are *Sand and Pearls* and *Voice of the Heart*. *Mither*, published in 2009, is a book of one hundred twenty-two story-poems, written in its entirety after Maxine suffered a left-side paralysis stroke. Her poems have continued to be published in the local Conway *Log Cabin Democrat* for over twenty-five years. Many of her poems have won prizes in poetry contests, appeared in Anthologies, and are on the Internet.

Maxine was a retired real estate broker, and a housewife. She was married to Carl for over sixty-one years. Maxine and her family made their home in Conway, Arkansas, for over thirty-eight years, where her husband and two daughters continue to reside.

Maxine passed away December 2, 2006, seven months and seven days after suffering a stroke. She left us with this rich legacy of poetry.

Poetic Potpourri is Maxine's fourth collection of published poetry. It represents a rich blend of poems in various forms with which Maxine loved to experiment.

Enjoy!

Foreword

Let a bit of Heaven touch your heart. If you have enjoyed reading *Sand And Pearls*, *Voice Of The Heart* and *Mither*, then *Poetic Potpourri*, Maxine's latest collection, is sure to please. May its fragrance of lovely poetic flowers blossom in your heart. In *Poetic Potpourri* is revealed the wisdom of the ages. You will gain new insight and perspective on life. Your spirit will soar to new heights, and with a deep satisfaction you will turn the last page.

Poetic Potpourri is a rich blend of the finest poems ever written. These poems are thought provoking, inspiring, and keenly perceptive into the foibles of human nature.

You will find a "remedy" for many problems and plights. Maxine always said, "God does not leave us without a remedy." So whatever your troubles or trials in life may be, she admonishes us all to "look up." These poems contain spiritual guidance, (the kind of love "seasoned with grace," that you read about in I Corinthians, chapter 13), along with philosophical thought and beautiful nature poems. Some are profound; some are just plain lovely.

Whatever your walk in life, you will be able to relate to these poems. You can't help but become a better, wiser person upon reading.

Maxine has reached a common denominator in human experience. We think everyone will agree that no one can say it better than Maxine. These poems are good food for thought, and beautiful flowers for the mind, heart and soul.

To all who knew her, Maxine's life exemplified all she wrote about. Nowhere could one find a more dedicated and faithful servant of the Lord. Maxine was a wonderful wife and mother. We're delighted to share her works with you.

May you have many hours of reading pleasure. You are sure to reach for this collection time and time again.

Although Maxine went home to Heaven to meet her full and great reward, her works live on as an example to the young, a source of consolation to the grieving, and a beacon of hope unto all. This is Maxine's rich legacy, of which we're privileged to be a part.

Glimpse the Heavenly within these covers, by this remarkable "woman of faith."

Affectionately, Maxine's two daughters,

Tena M. Hixon and Pamela Hixon Rhea

Haiku

Butterflies ...
Flying along together, a
Hanging garden

Table of Contents

God's Great Salvation 17
God's Clarion Call 18
Is Anything Too Hard for God? 19
Jesus was No Imposter ...
    but, Beware of Those Who Are! 20
Good and Evil (Triolet) 22
Only God is Good (Triolet) 22
Salvation's By Grace Through Faith (Triolet) 23
Tapestry of Life 24
All for Me! (Pantoum) 26
Ye are Epistles 27
We Don't Need to Challenge the devil 29
Whose Ox is Gored? 30
Faith Delivers 31
No Turning Back 32
Only Believe 34
Who is Man? 36
The True God 38
Pursue and Sue 39
Do You Love the Lord? Do You Really? 41
Eden Lost – Heaven Gained 42
Your Choice 43
A Mother's Legacy 44
Not Where ... but How 47
Parent or Peer? 49
What Legacy? 50
Then and Now 51
... Even a Child 52
Is it WWJD or 54
Training or Genes 55
Parents are Responsible (Triolet) 56
Lies (Triolet) 56

Good News and Bad News (Triolet)	57
On Patience (Triolet)	57
Character Does Count	58
God is to Be Feared	59
God's Way	61
God is More Than Able! (Triolet)	62
Not Thy Will, but Mine! (Triolet)	62
Something New (Triolet)	63
No Place to Hide (Triolet)	63
It's Priorities, Stupid (Triolet)	63
Truth Prevails	64
Love in Action (Cinquain)	66
In Its Own Time (Cinquain)	66
Vengeance Belongs to God (Cinquain)	66
Getting Back to the Basics	67
Changes From One-and-Twenty	68
Heaven Lost—Lucifer's Fall	69
... EXAMPLE ... or Would You Rather Be a JUDGE???	70
Like the Snowball	72
God So Loved (Triolet)	73
By Grace Through Faith (Triolet)	73
Summer Sun (Triolet)	74
Star of Winter (Triolet)	74
Help Us All	75
Diligence	76
There's a Reason	77
Light in the Dark	78
Matters Not – Night or Day (Rondeau)	79
Crooked Like a River	80
Somber Thoughts	81
Waiting	82
A Ruler	83
If Any Would Not Work ... Neither Should He Eat!	84
Death Knocks on Every Door	85
Why Wait?	86

Victory	86
Not Known!	86
Be First	86
Enjoy What You Can	87
Stop, Look and Listen!	87
Shhh … (Tanka)	87
Ode on Happiness	88
Choices	89
Heart to Heart	90
All Things …	91
A Tribute to Loving Dads	92
The Past	94
Easter Brings Hope	95
Easter and Springtime	96
A Different Perspective	97
Christmas in the Air	98
All Year Long	100
Christmas Means More Than Shopping and Spice	101
Do Your Worship the Lord, or the Christmas Tree?	102
A Gift of Love	103
Father's Day (Triolet)	104
When You Have Children of Your Own (Triolet)	104
Maybe and Maybe Not! (Cinquain)	105
Springtime (Cinquain)	105
Mother's Day (Triolet)	106
You're Mine	107
Valentine's Day? Everyday!	108
An Irish Valentine	109
Straight Shooter (Triolet)	110
Where's the Stuff? (Triolet)	110
Sunrise in Summer	111
Everything Going Wrong (Triolet)	112
Beauty Plus	113
Literary Sidewinders	114
Spring	115

Just Listen	115
Liliac Flowers (Triolet)	116
Butterflies (Triolet)	116
To Each His Own	117
Tanka – The birds ...	118
Tanka – As the rose ...	118
Tanka –Springtime!	118
Tanka –Though our sins ...	118
Never Seen	119
For All	119
Everything for Me!	119
Put God First	120
Too Late!	120
My Little Shadow	121
Sestina	123
The Mouse	125
They're Back!	127
The Cabbage Patch	128
A Vow is a Vow is a Vow! (Triolet)	129
Be Careful What You Vow! (Cinquain)	130
Forgotten (Limerick)	131
Unusual	132
An April Fools' Essay!	133
Keepsake (Triolet)	135
A Cutting (Triolet)	135
Just Take Time to Remember	136
Sweetheart, Another Anniversary	137
Anniversary! (Triolet)	138
God's Man (Triolet)	139
Time Change (Tanka)	140
True Love (Triolet)	141
Nostalgia	142
Memory Lane (Quatrain)	143
The Lilac	144
My Birthday	146

Another Year Older 147
January Twenty-Ninth 148
Barefoot Boy Turned Barefoot Man 149
Arkansas (Triolet) 153
Sandman 154
Triad 154
More Work! 154
Busy 155
So Wise 155
The Zebra 155
So Thankful He Cares 156
Time Does Tell (Villanelle) 157
An Even Place 158
A Way of Life 159
Responsibility 160
Triolet – When He Returned, He Brought Me a Ring 161
Triolet – When We Were Moving to the West Coast 161
Triolet – His Garden of Tulips is Beautiful 161
Triolet – He Loves All Kinds of Roses 161
Triolet – My Little Shadow is a Schipperke 162
Triolet – So Many Things I Love to Do! 162
Triolet – I Have Accepted Christ as My Saviour 162
Triolet – Love Should Rule the Home! 162
A Black Umbrella 163
Depression's Dark Umbrella 164
Matters Not, Little or Grown! (Terza Rima) 165
Coming or Going! 167
Standing Appointment (Limerick) 169
The Wimp (Limerick) 169
Fragile? (Limerick) 170
The Inevitable (Limerick) 170
Calories Can't Keep a Secret (Quatrain) 171
"Doctor, Doctor, Come Quick! Take a Closer Look" 172
Ode on Money 174
On the Money Trail (Tercet) 175

Trying You May Succeed! (Cinquain)	176
Who First? (Cinquain)	176
Together (Cinquain)	177
Repeat! (Cinquain)	177
It Took a Child	178
What If! (Triolet)	179
Oh Me! Oh My! (Triolet)	180
The Oyster (Triolet)	181
Slick Politicians	182
Like Feathers (Triolet)	183
Guilty, Also! (Triolet)	183
Flying High	184
Comeuppance	185
Cart Before the Horse	186
Senryu – Pawnshop	187
Senryu – The Twig	187
From Hand to Foot (Cinquain)	188
Smiling (Triolet)	188
Senyru – A Horse	189
Senryu – Let Another	189
Senryu – Don't Tell	189
Senryu –Money Earned	189
Senryu – Money Worked For	189
Haiku – The Wind	190
Haiku – Dark Moon	190
Senryu – Cold Outside	190
Senryu – A Baby!	190
Now … Don't Forget! (Cinquain)	191
Haiku – Spring Rains	191
Test Day! (Cinquain)	191
Haiku – Eyes Bright	192
Haiku – Smile	192
Haiku – Rosebush	192
Haiku – Cool Breeze	193
Haiku – So Quiet	193

Haiku – Tall Tales ... 193
Haiku – Black Out ... 193
Haiku – Cancel ... 193
Haiku – Lazy ... 194
Haiku – Deep Snow ... 194
Haiku – Not Hungry ... 194
Haiku – Snowfall ... 194
Haiku – Sunshine ... 194
Haiku – Acorn Falls ... 195
Haiku – Quiet Zone ... 195
Haiku – Tiny Ant ... 195
Haiku – Night Sky ... 195
Haiku – Gold Watch ... 195
Move On (Cinquain) ... 196
Two Ways (Cinquain) ... 196
All Mine! (Cinquain) ... 196
Haiku – Hands Sweep ... 197
Haiku – Good News ... 197
Haiku – The Canopy ... 197
Haiku – Bermuda Triangle ... 197
Haiku –The Rose ... 197
Before, Not After ... 198
What's in a Name? ... 199
Variety ... 200
Spirit Renewed ... 201
Real Love ... 203
When God Forgets ... 204
Another Year??? ... 206
My Family and I ... 207
My Prayer ... 209
My Savior Cares For Me ... 210
God's Love Never Fails ... 211
Believe the Lord ... 212
Storm Clouds of Life ... 213
Lord, Help Me ... 214

Life 215
The Savior's Love...............215
The Love of Money 216
Are You as Rich as I? 218

God's Great Salvation

God's Spirit searches the heart of man;
The Holy Spirit convicts again ...
From God there's nothing hidden can be;
The "All Seeing Eye," all things doth see.

When God searches each and every heart,
He's aware of depravity's part ...
Man born in sin, will have a Judgment call;
Christ died to save souls, after man's fall.

Accept Christ as Savior, ALL need do:
He's life's example ... we need pursue;
Anything short of perfection's, sin ...
On His righteousness, we must depend.

Asking forgiveness ... sins to confess;
Should fallen man expect to do less?
When a righteous God sent His only Son,
Bearing the loss ... to die on the cross.

There's Heaven to choose and Hell to shun:
Christ, the only way ... there's only one:
God made man a free moral agent ...
The choice is yours, the Sacrifice sent.

A home in Heaven, priceless, yet, free;
Christ paid sin's price on Calvary's tree:
Though Salvation's a gift proffered to all,
Many reject Christ ... heedless of call.

God's Clarion Call

God's clarion call to Salvation ... through Christ the
    Lord ...
Jesus came to save ... stated plainly in God's Holy
    Word —;
He of His own volition ... gave His life on the old
    rugged cross,
That all who believe might have their sins forgiven ...
    removing the dross.

God's clarion call to service ... after Salvation – never
    wavering in its sound ...
Work to do for the Savior ... if living in His favor –
    wherever man is found.
Serving the Lord ... in serving humanity ... wherever the
    need abounds ...;
The clarion call rings ever more clear ... for workers in
    His vineyard ... where acceptable service redounds.

Is Anything Too Hard for God?

God is love, and He is all-powerful;
There is one thing for man, God cannot do ...
He can't save a person against his will,
God will forgive, but cannot repent for you!

God's plan for Salvation is through the Lord;
It has never changed; always been the same;
Salvation is free ... works are for reward.
God made the stars and calls them all by name.

He made the earth and all that lies therein.
God created everything, then made man,
Put Adam and Eve in a garden to tend ...
The devil tricked Eve ... man fell into sin!

You think He doesn't know the hurt we bear!
Even the hairs on our head are numbered ...
God knows and can lift the burden of care.
With faith and obedience ... He's always there.

Jesus was No Imposter ...
but, Beware of Those Who Are!

(I John 2:22-23)

Religious zealots crucified God's Son:
Claiming He was an imposter ... from God didn't come!
He "gave" His life on Calvary to save the lost;
Why would an imposter pay such an awful cost?
The self-righteous Pharisees were struck on self,
A heart without Christ is of righteousness bereft!
God's Word says our "righteousness" is as filthy rags:
All who refuse to accept Christ ... the devil tags.

No matter the reports of "goodness" our own ...
The refusal of His Son ... God does not condone:
Water, steam and ice are all three H2O ...
God the Father, Holy Spirit and the Son
Is Heaven's Trinity ... three in one Godhead;
Those who accept Christ are of the Spirit led.
Pious imposters are out to deceive ...
Claiming to know God ... your vote to receive.

"Who is a liar, but he that denieth
That Jesus is the Christ? He is antichrist,
That denieth the Father and the Son."
God, the Father, Son and Holy Spirit are one!
"Whosoever denieth the Son the
Same hath not the Father ... he that acknowledgeth
The Son hath the Father, also ..." to know God
Once must come through ... Jesus, God's Son.

For one even to pray to God ... if you please ...
You must come through Christ by grace through faith and belief.
There are many imposters, but Jesus wasn't one.
All who fail to accept Him as their own Savior,
God will say, "Depart from me ye workers
Of iniquity ... for I never knew you ..."
"Whosoever denieth the Son, the same
Hath not the Father." I John 2:23

Good and Evil

(Triolet)

The devil is a liar and the father of it:
God is love, the devil EVIL ... only God is good!
God will have him cast into Hell, the burning pit,
The devil is a liar and the father of it:
Lucifer, a fallen archangel, found in Holy Writ:
He planned to exalt himself even above God;
The devil is a liar and the father of it:
God is love, the devil EVIL ... only God is good!

Only God is Good

(Triolet)

It's not by works of righteousness, which we have done,
But, according to His mercy ... hath He saved us ...
As it is written, "There's none righteous, no not one:"
It's not by works of righteousness, which we have done,
Jesus said, "There is none good but one; that is God."
Salvation comes by Grace through Faith when Christ you trust:
It's not by works of righteousness, which we have done,
But, according to His mercy ... hath He saved us.

Salvation's By Grace Through Faith

(Triolet)

Salvation is not of works, but by grace through faith,
Our righteousness is as filthy rages in God's sight:
Today's the day of Salvation ... why do you wait?
Salvation is not of works, but by grace through faith,
Accept Christ as your Savior before it's too late;
For whatsoever doth make manifest is light ...
Salvation is not of works, but by grace through faith:
Our righteousness is as filthy rags in God's sight.

Tapestry of Life

Tapestry is a heavy textile, handwoven with
    colored and undyed yarns;
Reversible – and of intricate – pictorial ...
    design.
The tapestry weaver – unlike the rug weaver –
    faces the back as he works, with his broche,
Pressing the stitches tightly – one against
    the other – to refine,
The colored "woof" yarns entirely cover
    the undyed "warp" – following the cartoon ...
Which is the pattern ...
Drawn by an artist –
    perhaps famous in his time.
Manifold uses for tapestry cloth ... spread
    widely – soon ...
Famous tapestries ... walls adorn, in churches,
    museums and palaces, fine.

As tapestry is reversible ... quality for each side
    is the same;
Tapestry in the weaving – is as a life in the process
    of living ...!
Needing – carefully to follow the "pattern" which is
    God's Holy Word.

As tapestry is reversible and either side gives pleasure –
    nothing to hide;
Our lives should be woven with threads of silver
    and gold ... righteousness to show;
Then it won't matter which side is shown –
    to the public – with Godly living.
When accepting Christ as Savior it's as if we start
    anew – undyed "warp" threads – the weaving's up to you.
Tangled in the weaving of our pattern – caught between
    the top and underside, on ourselves we can't rely!

God sees both sides of our weaving ... knowing
    every bobble and mistake!
Tells us to trust Him ... not waiting 'till all
    goes awry, for He seeks our best.
In taking time to study and pray ... to His
    Will we need awake.
Asking for guidance in the "patterns," the colors
    and the rest;
Obeying His Will ...weaving with Him
    choosing – from our own will break.
Eternal life is a gift – rewards are based on –
    will our weaving pass the reversible test?
When our tapestry is finished – at the close
    of day – our weaving ending in death!
The weaving's over – our tapestry is finished,
    either for good or bad ... then the judgment – yet!!

All for Me!

(Pantoum)

Because I was born in sin,
Totally depraved, as all humanity;
Christ came as the Redeemer;
For all have the Adamic nature.

Totally depraved as all humanity;
God sent His Son to die ...
For all have the Adamic nature;
He shed His blood on Calvary's Cross,

God sent His Son to die ...
For all who would accept Him as Savior;
He shed His blood on Calvary's Cross;
He'll save everyone who believes.

For all who would accept Him as Savior,
For by grace are ye saved through faith;
He'll save everyone who believes;
For this, God sent His Son into the world.

For by grace ye are saved through faith;
Not by works which we have done ...
For this, God sent His Son into the world;
Salvation's free to all who will believe;

Not by works which we have done ...
But, by Christ's righteousness we are saved,
Salvation's free to all who will believe,
It's a gift ... Christ paid the price.

But, by Christ's righteousness, we are saved;
Christ came as the Redeemer ...
It's a gift ... Christ paid the price.
Because I was born in sin.

Ye are Epistles

II Cor. 3:2, "Ye are epistles written in our hearts;
    Known and read of all men –."
... An epistle is a letter ...
What kind of a letter with our lives, do we start?
Many times, as we write on a piece of paper;
    And it doesn't turn out right –.
We crumple and throw away the letter;
    Putting it away out of sight!
Things read in our lives – not discarded as a piece of paper!
    We need repent ... make things right!
With God's forgiveness, making a new start;
Then be more careful with what ink we write.

Is it we get so busy in writing our epistle,
We take little heed as to how we write?
A letter – if possible – we'd like to say we didn't write?
Maybe something we didn't do just right!
And looking back – we'd like it kept out of sight!
Things at times – are awhile, in coming to light!
As with invisible ink – just for awhile out of sight!
Though our lives may resemble an open book;
But, that may not always be as it looks.
Since we are the one our own epistle to write;
Perhaps, things secret – not yet brought to light!
Remember this "invisible ink" doesn't make it all right!

                                  Continued

They will be brought to light – the Scripture is right!
There's a saying – "You can fool all the people
Part of the time – part of the people all the time
But, you can't fool God any of the time."
There's One we can never deceive – try as we might.
He sees everything – all is done – in His sight.
Invisible to all others for awhile it may seem;
But, no matter how pious we tend to lean;
Our epistle is read – actions speak louder than words.
If there's a blot of invisible ink still – our plight.
In judgment – reading will be done in God's light,
One needs be careful how with our lives we write.

We Don't Need to Challenge the devil

We are never to challenge the devil;
Even the angels dared not to accuse him ...
Nor railings against angels who fell
We are never the challenge the devil.
Our great God will cast him into Hell!
We are never to challenge the devil;
Even the angels dare not accuse him.
Though we are weak ... Christ is strong.
We are told to say, "Get thee behind me satan" – not to challenge.
The angels are not to bring railings or accusations against him.
When he detained Gabriel twenty-one days, God sent Michael to aid in the battle.
Gabriel and Michael are archangels ... it took both of them.
The Bible is filled with examples, telling of the strength of angels.
We are made a little lower than the angels; in the flesh, we are weak,
And no match for the devil, the archangel who fell.
Remembering our weakness ... God's help always seek.
No challenge is necessary to get the devil's attention.
He is busy twenty-four hours a day, hounding God's creation.
He leads the lost into Hell, and can ruin the saved's testimony.
Only through Christ, can victory be won.

Whose Ox is Gored?

Are you the type? ... Are you one of them?
If it isn't your ox ... your understanding's dim!
You may be overlooked this time ...
Just down the road your own obstacle you'll find.
Don't ever be guilty of pushing out of sight,
Something you know is wrong ... and can't be right!

Next time around ... perhaps you can't say,
"No concern of mine – no dog in that fight belongs to me."
If it's your ox that's gored – then what'll it be?
On principle ... it matters not – my ox or yours – you see;
Others have feelings and could use some help;
While we just trudge away and with evil fall in step;

No doubt if this attitude you take,
You'll soon find the detour was a mistake;
Chickens have a way of coming home to roost;
That many times over ... will cook your goose.
Good advice – stand true to God and right as best you can;
Just lamenting your "own ox ..." isn't really taking a stand!

Faith Delivers

The wicked flee when no man pursueth,
While the righteous are as bold as lions.
As a man thinketh in his heart, so is he ...
Without faith, it's impossible to please God.

Three Hebrew children in a fiery furnace ...
Because of their faith, God delivered them.
Christ was there among the flames ... giving grace;
Daniel's faith saved him from the lion's den.

God's Word says: "Buy the truth and sell it not!"
In the time we live ... TRUTH is auctioned cheap:
It's Heaven or Hell ... man chooses his lot ...
Man turning from the truth, trouble does reap.

God made man a little lower than angels.
God has a plan for redeeming the lost;
It's by grace through faith in Christ, His Word tells:
A gift of God ... not of works ... no one can boast!

No Turning Back

Luke 9:62, Jesus said unto him, "No man, having put
his hand to the plow and looking back, is fit for
the kingdom of God." ... (for service in the labors
of the kingdom of God, if one has an unstable world-loving
attitude or disposition)

When a man repeatedly looks back while plowing,
The row he plows is inevitably crooked ...
Israel looked back to Egypt's onions and garlic;
While heavenly manna was before their eyes!

Before salvation, all are children of wrath ...
Times past, lived ... fulfilling desires of the flesh
And of the mind; refusing the narrow path;
God, rich in mercy ... by His Spirit drew us.

For it's a shame even to speak of those things
Done in secret before salvation brought light;
Whose God is their belly ... whose glory, their shame;
Who mind earthly things ... for in this, they delight.

God gave His Son to die for us on the cross:
Through Christ, raised us up by His own matchless grace,
Christ willingly gave His life to save the lost;
His blood blots out all past sins ... leaving no trace.

As did Paul ... forget those things which are behind,
And reaching forth to those things which are before ...
Press toward the mark for the prize of the high
Calling of God in Christ ... always trusting more.

When saved, we're not our own, for Christ paid the price,
We're to bring honor to God and Christ who died:
In charity, spirit, faith and purity ...
An example in word and manner of life.

The love of money's the root of ALL evil!
Since God knows of everything His children need,
Let us be free from the LOVE of money ...
Plowing straight ... not looking back, sowing good seed.

For the fruit of the Spirit is peace, joy, love,
Longsuffering, gentleness, goodness and faith,
Meekness, temperance, against such there is no law.
They that are Christ's, have crucified the flesh with ...

The affections and lusts ... Paul's advice is to put
Away every weight and sin which so easily ...
Beset us ... run with patience the Christian race;
Don't turn back, but by faith, plow straight, that not seen.

Only Believe

All things are possible to him that believeth ...
In Christ's name, we need ask with faith, help to
    receive;
We must trust God to provide what's needed in
    life,
Trusting in faith while dark threads with bright
    ones He weaves.

He'll not put more on us than we're able to bear:
As the Master weaver ... God knows, just what we
    need ...
To obey Him in adversity ... we should dare;
To prove our love should be, not in words ...
    but by deeds.

Walking by sight ... in light of the sun, is not
    faith;
But, it's pressing on, through dark, black shadows
    of night ...
Serving as best we can ... faith bright, end not
    in sight;
Letting Christ shine in our lives ... the world's
    only light.

In prayer, if we waver in faith, God will not
 hear ...
Nor, if we regard iniquity in our heart:
God's Word teaches, He alone, is the one to
 fear:
Christ is the Way ... in Salvation, works have
 no part.

Salvation is free ... Christ suffered for me and
 you;
By repentance and faith, Christ can be your
 Savior,
A choice you make ... choosing is the only part
 you do;
For Salvation's by grace through faith ... not
 works ... in lieu!!!

It's Heaven or Hell, and you will choose while
 living ...
God did not made man ... a puppet, but a free moral
 agent;
Jesus died to save the lost ... His own life,
 giving;
For my sin and your sin ... on the cross, Christ
 was rent.

Who is Man?

The Ten Commandments are part of God's law,
Moses received them, God's face never saw;
The law was given to the children of Israel,
The New Testament teaches morals the same.

Some want changed laws to cover seeds they've sown;
Some that won't condemn ... God's they have outgrown;
Things going well, no need on God to call ...
Forgetting! Anytime, God can change it all!

What of the next generations that be?
Those gone before ... lax morals ... are what they see;
With the permissive examples and teaching they get,
Just look what we've come to, and end ... isn't yet!

Discipline in the home and schools is antiquated;
The courts and judge make the rules ... so stated!
To enforce God's moral law, there is no will ...
A Spiritual moral gap ... man can never fill.

Train up a child in the way he should go ...
When he is old, he will not depart from it;
That's a loving God's way ... He isn't our foe.
We're God's creation ... yet, many choose woe.

God so loved the world, He sent Christ to die;
Many refuse Christ; Salvation by works ... try;
Christ died on the cross that we might be saved;
He shed His blood, and life He freely gave.

Man dishonors God to exalt himself ...
Just think! Without God, where would man be left?
In love, God gave His only begotten Son—
The Redeemer will be a Judge, when life is done.

Who is man, that Thou art mindful of him?
God's "All Seeing Eye," looks on evil's trend;
God's love extends Salvation to everyone;
For you, He sacrificed His own dear Son.

There are those who declare a "New" set of rules ...
Is needed everywhere and in our schools!
When IF it weren't for God's kindness and love;
ALL who oppose Him would be struck from above.

Any with beliefs that oppose the Lord ...
The devil's their master – Hell ... their reward;
The Ten Commandments were God's law to give ...
They are still the BEST rules by which to live.

The True God

Our God is the Creator of ALL things:
He is not fashioned by man's feeble hands;
Which possessors thrash, demanding amends ...
This truly has happened ... in heathen lands.

Christian people, this, just can't comprehend;
Taking stock of our lives ... should this be so?
When there are many false "gods" we defend ...
Putting them in God's place ... not saying, "no."

Whatever we allow to come between ...
Us and service to our God, proves the same;
As the heathenish practice we deem ...
So unbelievable ... though a "silly" game.

We're to have no other gods before us!
NO OTHER! And not only a few so named!
The True and Living God in whom we trust,
Is the ONLY GOD ... worshipped without blame.

God is the giver of everything good ...
Blessings shouldn't have first place in the heart:
No one can come between ... as many would,
When God comes first ... and not the "blessing" part.

"Thou shalt have no other gods before me ..."
Was the command our Great God gave to man;
From His love flows every blessing we see,
We're to WORSHIP Him ... not blessings demand!

Happy is the man whose God is the Lord:
A double-minded man is unstable in ...
All his ways ... God's Word is a two-edged sword,
Cutting straight ... to convict man of all sin.

Pursue and Sue

(I Corinthians 6:19)

Man's body is the temple of the Lord ...
When Christ dwells in a heart ... this abode is His;
Every abusive substance man can hoard,
Fills God's temple ... making it what it is.

A puff here and a puff there, with fresh air combine,
Yet, not all from chimneys as one might think ...
But, from smokers outside their houses ... rain or shine;
Smoking inside makes the air inside stink!

Breathing fresh air is better for your health!
There's no one ... who doesn't know this is true:
Staying healthy even adds to a person's wealth;
Lungs need protection ... we only have two!

Continued

Though lungs saturated with nicotine ...
Can cause a sickness that's sometimes terminal;
While air inside the house smells nice and clean:
The things once enjoyed are as though unseen.

While lungs are essential in life to breathe,
More thought given to walls and upholstery;
If lungs could give an opinion ... they'd seethe!
Demanding fresh air ... since God made it free ...

If abused lungs appeared before Congress ...
Lobbying for fresh air ... God gave for free;
All the officials would call for a recess;
As the protestors march, they'd try to flee.

After some have smoked for most of their lives;
Though health is gone ... still their habit pursue ...
Then there's a lawsuit before hearing the fife:
The sum or gist ... look what you made me do!

Do You Love the Lord?
Do You Really?

All things work together for good
To those who love the Lord and are
Called according to His purpose ...
God's plan ... man's weakness, cannot mar.

God hath chosen the foolish things
Of the world to confound the wise;
And weak things to shame the mighty.
God's strength can never be denied.

Many recorded examples ...
In God's word ... proving this is right;
Little is much when God's in it,
For God has all power and might.

Even bad times can turn to good,
When God is working His "purpose;"
If ... loving the Lord as we should,
Only what's good can come to us.

We need do as God commands us ...
And then we have nothing to fear;
He'll care for us if we will trust;
For His children to Him are dear.

As troubles come ... filling our life,
For a time, obscuring Heaven's light;
Have faith, though wounded, as with a knife:
Just love the Lord ... He'll make things right.

Eden Lost – Heaven Gained

Eve's sorrow was multiplied – in conception.
She allowed her rebellion to get out of hand.
Her desire – be to her husband, because of her defection.
And he is to rule over her – in the land.
Adam was not deceived – eyes open – his election!
The ground was cursed because of Adam, the man.
In sorrow he toils to bring forth food; his rejection.
Mist thorns and thistles, as best he can.
Ever since, thus – the lot – because of man's election.
If Adam and Eve would have given heed,
To instructions given them of God;
They could have eaten of the Tree of Life;
Instead of the Tree of Knowledge – discerning bad and what was good.
They made their choice – separated from God, having to die!

Adam and Eve having freedom of choice – disobeyed! "Eden Lost."
If they had chosen right ...
They'd have lived forever in a blissful state.
God placed at the east of the Garden of Eden, cherubims;
With flaming swords turning as He bade.
Keeping man in his sinful state from the Tree of Life!
Warning: To all who believe the devil they can make pay
On their own, like Adam and Eve, cause nothing but strife;
Only by faith in Christ we escape hell's pit; "Heaven Gained."
We have the Bible – no excuse – excuses are rife.
Let us read and study God's Holy Writ.
Stand for what's right, be heard – definitely as the fife!
Allow our lives, with God's spirit to be lit;
Yielding our life to the Great One – not husband or wife.

Your Choice

... Joshua admonished the children of Israel –
    and shouldn't have been ignored ...
"Choose ye this day ... whom you will serve ..." hearts
    should have stirred ...
"But, as for me and my house ..." a decision he made ...
    "We will serve the Lord;"
All the past great things God had done for their
    nation, from their fathers had already heard.

They only reiterated all things God had brought
    their nation through in the past;
That wasn't choosing ... that was reminiscing of truths
    taught by their fathers of old ...
God requires more than repeating a history lesson –
    he requires faith that lasts —;
Choosing the true God to serve ... not turning aside
    to false gods ... as Joshua's example told.

Joshua not only chose for himself ... the way that
    was true —;
He made the choice for his house ... they would all
    serve the Lord ...
Many ask how can this be ... each individual his own
    course — must pursue —;
Joshua, being head of his house had a responsibility;
    with recompense to the reward.

God holds parents responsible for the children
    He loans —;
For so much more than just material needs as
    clothing, shelter and food;
We are only caregivers for our children ... we do
    not own ...
Parenting is a full-time job – caring, teaching ...
    ALWAYS, not just when we're in the mood.

A Mother's Legacy

(Lo, children are an heritage of the
 Lord: and the fruit of the womb is
 His reward.) Psalms 127:3

Our children are on loan from God,
For their care we'll answer to Him;
"Old fashioned" parents ... are not "mod!"
God's Word teaches how to raise them.

In the nurture and admonition ...
Of the Lord ... to parents, a command:
A job considered menial to some;
Missing the accolades so grand!

Listening for their cry, day and night;
Not nine to five, but, sun to sun ...
Making light of what some call plight,
Still, making time to join their fun.

Always lodged in a true mother's heart,
Is teaching them what's good and right;
An obligation ... she feels her part ...
God's love always the depth and height.

The precepts of the Lord when learned,
Will be recalled in later life ...
Whether in lowly circumstance
Or exalted ... with honor's rife.

Faith in Christ should be taught early;
It's never too soon to start ...
When understanding comes in time,
Love of Christ fills each tender heart.

When they are taught so soon from birth,
Teaching with words they understand;
That Jesus is the best of friends:
He died to save the soul of man;

As years pass, their faith will increase,
When taught at first what's important;
Faith won't always make troubles cease;
But, will give strength to make them stand.

Childhood lullabies sometimes soothe,
At times, so does rocking in a chair;
Security is in knowing Christ ...
And the Holy Spirit is near.

Man is few days ... full of trouble,
And they culminate with the years ...
Still, a life can be lived to the full;
With faith in God, to calm life's fears.

A Mother's love will show in children,
By values she instills in them ...
Accepting Christ as their Savior;
They'll spend eternity with Him.

Continued

Doing her best with what she has,
Providing for those in her care ...
Trusting in God to see them through;
Love goes where nothing else will dare.

Circumstances can't confine love;
Where there's faith, there is no limit.
Such love as this is from above ...
And though a lifetime ... seems like minutes.

A soft silk dress or suit of fine serge,
Though nice, will soon be ragged and worn;
Where Scriptures will in memory verge ...
Guiding one who has been reborn.

When small they learned John 3:16,
Saying it when first they could talk;
Was a part of education deemed ...
Later to help life's maze to walk.

To protect them is love's design;
In Christ, they're covered by His blood:
All evil ... the devil's behind ...
But, his power's checked by God above.

A Mother's legacy is what she's taught:
To her children ... her life does speak;
In good times, or through hardships wrought,
Where with faith, it's God's Will she seeks.

Not Where ... but How

Our children are of great importance;
Not where we live ... but how?
Teaching values based on what's right;
Not putting off ... but NOW.

Living in a mansion or shack ...
Isn't what matters ... most –
It's where the heart ... always looks back;
... To home ... where it can boast.

Differs not ... what city or state ...
But, love in the family –
Within four walls ... casting out hate;
Love, in home ... all should see.

Unrest comes from lives ... not a place;
When family love's missing –
A family with love as its base;
Togetherness ... a blessing.

Continued

Drawn together ... serving the Lord;
Unselfishly ... caring ...
A little of Heaven ... on earth –
Each, life's burdens sharing.

Trouble lurks ... it will come to all;
Seeing it through ... matters ...
Bound in love ... with faith in the Lord;
Doubts ... will need scatter.

Not liking weather or taxes;
We complain about such ...
Our standing with the Lord ... fact is –
Is what matters so much.

A life, submissive, to the Lord;
Is one to Him we give ...
Serving in LOVE ... not for reward;
It's our will ... how we live.

Parent or Peer?

All parents have responsibilities:
To correct, protect, teach, chasten and love,
Acting not as a peer, but as a parent should;
Their place positioned ... under God above.

A liberal parent wants to be a child's best friend,
With no discipline ... remaining a child with them;
On someone mature, a child needs to depend ...
They need learn of the Lord ... learn to trust Him.

To be a mature parent ... liberals do fear:
Fearful from child's "good graces" they will fall;
They need adults with good morals ... not a peer,
Yet, God's standard condemns us one and all!

Children are a heritage of the Lord ...
To parents they are on loan ... they don't own;
The fruit of the womb is the Lord's reward:
Since they are His ... teaching right is due Him.

We're to chasten our children while there's hope,
And let not the soul spare for their crying;
We're to train a child in the way he should go:
And when old, he will not depart from it.

An old adage for generations heard ...
"Proof of the pudding is in the eating:"
A man's life is known by the standard he keeps;
The "proof" other evidence defeating.

What Legacy?

There's much talk about leaving a legacy,
And little preparation toward it ...
So many lies in talk and actions seen;
Digging deeper the all-engulfing pit.

All people, a good or bad example set,
So easily children follow in steps;
Making everyone in the children's debt,
Good morals are better than all tears wept.

Politicians share a large part of the blame,
For not keeping their word in, "speeches" made;
Young people see words and deeds not the same,
Faced with the truth – their confidence does fade.

It matters not whom the adult may be ...
They are the best example some child knows:
Where everything one does is known or seen,
With influence lost, becomes a tinkling cymbal!

God-fearing people with integrity ...
Will leave the children a priceless legacy;
Where our Lord is worshipped as deity,
Not selfishness, as ... I, myself and me!

Then and Now

Where are the brave ones ...
    who value God's ways and what's right?
Those who not thinking of self ... carry God's standard forth —;
Bearing the banner for Christ ... lighting a part
    of the night;
As sin's shadow fills the earth ... reaching from
    west, south, east and north.

Way back when ... conditions of sin now exist as then ...
Many offered their children for sacrifice to the
    heathen god molech ... causing such pain —;
A statue made of metal, made to him ... heated from
    within ... to burn in its arms, unable to defend.
Abortion is of the same ... partial birth ... so cruel
    and all so inhumane.

If we bid God's speed to evildoers – God's word says
    we're partakers of their evil deeds;
Not standing for right ... refusing to shine God's light ...
We'll not escape God's "All Seeing Eye" ... if failing
    to try ... taking no heed;
Those who stand for right ... will be upheld by God's
    Almighty Might.

Is nothing sacred anymore ... not even the sanctity
    of life?
Oh, when our lives are over ... What good will we have done?
Will we have made the world where strife is rife ...
A better place by living a life ... honoring God and
    our Savior, His only begotten Son???

... *Even a Child* ...

"Even a child is known by his doings, whether
    his work be pure, and whether it be right."
(Proverbs 19:11)

In a little town, not far away,
Tragedy struck ... a terrible day!
Before it struck, something went wrong;
When brought to light, many lives gone.

Whether town or in large cities,
Drive-bys, ambush ... shooting, one pities;
Much teaching needed, one must face:
Church, schools, may teach, but HOME'S the base.

Evil hidden, and then brought to light ...
Only exposed when at its height!
When it's too late ... remedy's sought;
Born in sin, life with dangers fraught,

The devil ruins each life he can ...
Busy is he ... each life to scan:
Doing his best, his trap he sets;
Unwary caught ... then there's regret.

Jesus, the WAY, the TRUTH, and LIFE:
Other teachings, in world are rife ...
Salvation comes ... no other way!
Christ at Calvary, for sin did pay.

When hearts are right, then lives will change;
NOT resolutions ... rearranged ...
Christ saves those, who on His name call;
Man transgressed ... into sin did fall.

What examples, the children see ...
Evil rampant, all must agree!
In many lives, little restraint;
Where good morals ... appear so quaint.

Flaunting sin ... good morals reject,
Makes for a people, whose lives are a wreck!
If children, to the Lord aren't led ...
We've failed our Lord, when all is said.

Standing in Judgment ... one day soon;
Our life finished, reaching our doom.
In Heaven or Hell, each will dwell!
With Christ your Savior, all is well.

Proverbs 19:18 "Chasten thy son while there is hope, and let not thy soul spare for his crying."

Is it "WWJD" or is it "What Would Jesus Not Do??"

Jesus would not do what many who wear these WWJD bracelets do,
    Or go where many who wear these bracelets go!
God's word says to keep ourselves unspotted from the world.
Studying God's word helps one God's Will to know.
After accepting Christ as Savior, the Holy Spirit helps one evil to discern.

Jesus would not wear the popular WWJD shirt and shorts,
The Bible tells of those whose God is their belly and glory their shame.
Jesus would not partake of any sin of the flesh or be a cohort,
We can't say "the devil made me do it ..." we stand the blame.

In temptation ... Jesus said, "My grace is sufficient,"
He will not allow us to be tempted above what we are able to stand.
Covetousness, drugs, alcohol, cards, dancing, adultery, lying and stealing
    Are the devil's tools ... just a few.
We are drawn away of our own lusts ... but the Lord will make a way of escape.

None of the sins of the flesh mentioned above gives God any glory,
If you think they do ... please explain how.
God's Word tells us to do all things to the glory of God
Whether we eat or drink or whatsoever we do!

Many things Jesus would do ... and many He would not do!
He would not neglect to witness to the lost,
He would not do many of the things His people pursue.
Jesus did God's Will ... no matter the cost.

Jesus is the same yesterday, today and forever!
Moral precepts in God's Word ... forever the same.

Training or Genes

(Proverbs 29:15)

The rod and reproof give wisdom;
A child left to himself brings shame:
Shame to the mother, who bore him,
"Genes," not mentioned as to the blame.

Many defects ... said caused by genes:
Train a child the way it should go ...
For Biblical ... that is the means;
Values instilled ... wearing the, "jeans."

Too much is placed on genetics,
Letting go much else on life's way;
God's way, with error will not mix ...
Teaching Christ ... will hold much at bay.

God's way, always the best ... is deemed;
"Spare the rod, spoil the child, brings shame:
Not, "genes ..." but rod's meant for the "jeans!"
Much gone awry ... parents to blame.

More than color of eyes and hair;
For training has a greater part:
Parents responsible for care ...
Teaching when young, the place to start.

Training a child with "genes" in "jeans;"
Takes discipline, with love ... the ... pair ...
"Genes," have a smaller part, it seems:
God's word, the instruction ... who'll dare?

Parents are Responsible

(Triolet)

Parents are responsible for their children,
    Not the country, state or village!
Parents are responsible for their children,
Children should know on them to depend,
    From very young or an older age,
Parents are responsible for their children,
    Not the country, state or village!

Lies

(Triolet)

You hate those afflicted by your lies,
    The Lord hates a lying tongue,
To stay with the truth is wise,
You hate those afflicted by your lies,
The truth, any refuting defies,
    Lies ruin a life, old or young.
Your hate those afflicted by your lies,
    The Lord hates a lying tongue.

Good News and Bad News

(Triolet)

There's some good news, and there's bad news;
Bad news ... the good news doesn't last!
But, things can get worse as we muse ...
There's some good news, and there's bad news;
We're not to think ALL good ... our dues;
Man is few days and full of trouble ...
There's some good news, and there's bad news;
Bad news ... the good news doesn't last!

On Patience

(Triolet)

If you earnestly pray for patience;
Why be surprised, when trouble comes?
Tribulation worketh patience ... Romans 5:3;
If you earnestly pray for patience ...
Man born of woman ... never trouble free;
Man is few days and full of trouble ... Job 14:1;
If you earnestly pray for patience;
Why be surprised when trouble comes?

Character Does Count

Character does count ...
And to all that's born;
Respect must be earned;
Garnering not free;
Suspicion does mount;
When the truth is scorned;
With lies come concern –
Not hidden ... to see.

To those afflicted;
By lies, another's told;
Hate by lies ... revealed;
The Bible says so!
Some to lies addicted;
Telling very bold ...
Best their lips were sealed;
Lies to friend and foe;
The devil's wicked.

Character does matter;
Everyone does know ...
You have a choice;
Choose for right or wrong;
Sin always scatters;
While truth onward goes;
Wisdom does rejoice;
Right triumphs long!!!

God is to Be Feared

"The angel of the Lord encamps all around
Those who fear Him ...
And delivers them;" with great power does surround
To protect them.

Sin in a life causes doubt, and faith will falter,
Turning from God ...
God's Holy Spirit does hearts convict and stir;
Of sin does prod.

Man being a free moral agent, must choose in life
How he will live ...
To accept or reject Christ, he must decide:
His choice to give.

The valley of death leads to eternity,
Each must travel:
Salvation, by grace through faith, to ALL is free;
The "field's" level!

Continued

"It's level the playing field ..." so many cry
Across our land ...
Christ died on the cross, God's plan none can defy;
Nor any can!

Choices man makes decides quality of life:
Trusting the Lord ...
Or in doubt, looking to the arm of the flesh,
For his reward.

Repentance and faith toward Christ, a soul is won;
Christ does the rest ...
Not by works of righteousness which we have done
  ... Be it our best.

To be pleasing to God, there has to be faith,
With Godly fear ...
God's children, who fear Him, and everyone, ought:
Angels are near.

God's Way
(Rondeau)

Good thoughts keep the heart and mind sound:
Right thinking taught, in Bible found ...
Philippians 4:8 tells what to think ...
True, honest, just, pure, lovely ... whatsoever are
Of good report ... of virtue and praise.

God can give one over to reprobate mind ...
Means corrupt ... good sense left behind;
God not retained in their knowledge ...
Good thoughts keep the heart and mind sound.
Repentance and faith ... upon Him lean;
God's children need to keep minds clean:

Washing of mind ... reading God's word;
Continue in prayer ... with hearts much stirred,
Will help us all ... time to redeem ...
Good thoughts keep the heart and mind sound.

God is More Than Able!
(Triolet)

God's able to do abundantly more than we ask or think:
We're told, without faith, it's impossible to please God;
In Salvation ... one of the water of life freely drinks,
God's able to do abundantly more than we ask or think:
Christ, in Salvation, rescues the lost from Hell's brink;
God so loved the world He gave Christ to die, man of the sod.
God's able to do abundantly more than we ask or think:
We're told, without faith, it's impossible to please God.

Not Thy Will, but Mine!
(Triolet)

Though we pray, "Not my will, but Thine,"
Then set to work ... our will be done,
We desire not, "Thy will but mine!"
Though we pray, "Not my will, but Thine,"
While sin and doubt in heart combine,
Not trusting all to God's own Son;
Though we pray, "Not my will, but Thine,"
Then set to work ... our will be done.

Something New
(Triolet)

To some folks, what's new, always seems the best;
Bible remains the same ... will never change ...
There are some, who from God's truth won't digress.
To some folks, what's new, always seems the best;
Eagerly waiting, the old, to divest ...
Multitudes caught up, when teachings are strange;
To some folks, what's new, always seems the best;
Bible remains the same ... will never change.

No Place to Hide
(Triolet)

Man is never able to hide from God:
While that which hides God from man's, an idol!
Compared to God, man is a worm of the sod;
Man is never able to hide from God:
To exalt God is not considered mod ...
Christ as Savior, to the soul, is vital!
Man is never able to hide from God:
While that which hides God from man's, an idol!

It's Priorities, Stupid!
(Triolet)

Love of money's the root of ALL evil:
Yet, there is no virtue in poverty!
It's priorities, stupid ...! Young or feeble,
Love of money's the root of ALL evil:
Though has its place even midst God's people,
A medium of exchange is all it should be ...
Love of money's the root of ALL evil:
Yet, there is no virtue in poverty!

Truth Prevails

If not at first ... truth will prevail;
God's in control of all ...
ALL answer to God without fail;
As JUDGE ... each name He'll call.

David prayed God not let his enemies ...
Have triumph over him —;
More prayer we need, down on our knees;
Victory is God's ... He will win.

God always keeps His word to us;
How do we answer Him ...
Do we obey without a fuss?
Or does our faith grow dim!

Christ came that we might all have life;
Have it more abundantly ...
When we obey, there is less strife;
A joyous life there'll be.

Failing to enjoy life God gives;
Is truly our own fault ...
Troubles will come ... long as one lives;
Only death ... brings a halt.

When one thinks truth's pushed aside;
Not for long ... that is true ...
God, being the Judge ... He will abide;
All wrong ... He will subdue.

No matter what others may think;
God misses no detail ...
At sin, His eye never does wink;
Truth and right will prevail.

If you don't have Christ as Savior;
When death knocks at your door ...
Suffering ... forever ... just begins;
Biblical ... not folklore.

Love in Action
(Cinquain)

God is
Love ... but teaches
In His Word; an eye for
An eye ... vengeance is mine saith ...
The Lord.

In Its Own Time
(Cinquain)
Ecclesiastes 3:8

There is
A time to love,
And there's a time to hate;
There's a time of war, and a time ...
Of peace.

Vengeance Belongs to God
(Cinquain)

Righteous
Indignation
Is not revenge ... vengeance
Is mine saith the Lord and I will ...
Repay!

Getting Back to the Basics
(Luke 6: 36-38)

The Bible teaches, be ye merciful,
Condemn not, and ye shall not be condemned:
To forgive and ye shall be forgiven;
Also, to judge not, that ye be not judged.

"Give and it shall be given unto you,
Good measure, pressed down, shaken together,
And running over, shall men give into
Your bosom ... for it's with the same measure,

That ye mete withal it shall be measured
To you again..." reaping that which we sow!
When hate and resentment's stored and treasured,
It acts as a "canker" to you, not the foe.

In "self pity" ... martyrs we'll ALL soon be;
Forever wronged, in our own estimation ...
  ... But, what does our God's "All Seeing Eye" see?
We answer to him ... there's no other one.

Repentance is God's plan, helps keep a sound mind;
Forgiveness only comes when hearts are right ...
Though born depraved ... sin can be put behind:
Because of God's gift, Christ's death, love and might.

Changes From One-and-Twenty

At one-and-twenty, secure;
    A few years later – dread,
Youth with ease will still endure,
    The hardships that were said.
Resiliency pushes aside
    Troubles that never cease,
Optimism still abides,
    Young brow that naught does crease.

Years escape the other side,
    Residue only left;
Life so spent on highways wide,
    Of lasting things bereft.
Life's setting sun sinking low,
    We meet the Savior soon,
Neglect of right – life's great foe,
    Without Christ, Hell and doom.

Remember Christ in your youth,
    Old age has less to rue;
God's grace keeps from us our due,
    Salvation's free ... it's true.
Young or old, it matters not,
    Christ died to pay the price;
God's plan will not change one jot,
    God's Way is plain ... concise.

Heaven Lost – Lucifer's Fall

Lucifer was not satisfied with his earthly
 dominion.
One of God's archangels was he – there were
 three.
The earth was the territory over which he
 ruled.
He wanted greater power – to be like God, you
 see.
Lucifer said, "I will ascend above the heights of
 the clouds;
I will exalt my throne above the stars of
 God.
I will be like the most high." But God,
 said,
"Lucifer, son of the morning, How art
 thou
Cut down to the ground, which did waken
 the nations!
For thou hast said in thine heart;
 'I will
Ascend into heaven,' Yet, thou shalt be
 brought
Down to hell, to the sides of the
 pit."

... EXAMPLE ...
or *Would You Rather Be a* JUDGE???

There used to be strict moral requirements
For teachers ... even given ... a dress code:
Restrictions vanquished for women and men;
What's "mod" may not be decency's, "mode."

As reading, writing, arithmetic ...
Per se ... do not on good things lay hold;
The three, "R's" as known, won't do the trick,
While good examples stand out so bold!

It's been said, "Education's lacking
When there is no knowledge of God's word:"
"Do as I say ... not as I do ..." rings
In ears ... an old adage, all have heard.

Respect must be earned ... isn't a right:
With what judgment you judge, you'll be judged,
Measured to you again is ... what you mete ...
It behooves each, from judging to budge.

Thou which teachest another teachest
Thou not thyself? A man should not steal!
Does thou steal after what thou preaches ...
A good example will do much to heal.

It's been said, "The more strict parents or
Teachers were, the most headstrong children,
Who have forgotten, how sin can mar ...
Turning from what help they could have been."

Why beholdest thou the mote that is
In thy brother's eye, but considereth
Not the beam that is in THINE own eye?
Matthew 7:3 ... we do resist!!!

The "Mote" is only some speck ... you see
Magnified, many times over ...
While in thine "own eye" ... is a Log, called a "beam:"
Much more easily seen ... as it were!!!

Parents, teachers ... should be examples ...
Leading children, to accept the Lord ...
So much difference in lives they could make;
Lives given to Christ ... reap great reward.

Like the Snowball

One lie – two lies – three lies – four ... with the
    telling of one – there'll need be more;
Thinking to obscure or cover what's already been
    said ...
A "pack of lies," isn't folklore ... for in the telling
    of one – then seeing a "pack" has gone ... before;
In telling the truth, and to the truth if wed – a person
    will find – always to come out ahead.

We've heard the saying – something is "snowballing ..."
    when getting out of hand;
The Bible says, the tongue is a fire – a world of iniquity –
    and setteth on fire the course of nature, and it is set on
    fire of hell. (James 3:6)
Telling the truth is much simpler – not trying to remember
    what was told before – with questions galore – with a
    right to demand.
As the "snowball" rolls – gaining in momentum as it increases
    in size ... so do a multitude of lies burn helter–skelter
    ... pell-mell!

God So Loved
(Triolet)

God so loved the world,
    He sent His Son to die.
By Adam, the world into sin was hurled,
God so loved the world,
God's plan for redemption, in Christ unfurled
    His death at Calvary, is where it lies.
God so loved the world,
    He sent His Son to die.

By Grace Through Faith
(Triolet)

By grace through faith, we are saved.
    It's a gift of God, and not by works.
When accepting Christ as Savior, our sin is waived.
By grace through faith, we are saved.
We're born in sin, our nature depraved!
    The devil's aim is to ruin lives – close he lurks.
By grace through faith, we are saved.
It's a gift of God, and not by works.

Summer Sun
(Triolet)

The summer sun is sometimes too warm,
    Yet, can be soothing and healing.
Too much at once can do much harm.
The summer sun is sometimes too warm.
With no hat, in places, brings alarm,
    To be caught out, a terrible feeling.
The summer sun is sometimes too warm,
    Yet, can be soothing and healing.

Star of Winter
(Triolet)

The evergreen's the Star of Winter,
    Time now for budding, flowering trees.
Into fall, some will linger,
The evergreen's the Star of Winter.
Ice and snow to them do not hinder,
    When winds blow hard and there's a freeze.
The evergreen's the Star of Winter
    Time now for budding, flowering trees.

Help Us All

Dear Lord ... I ask your help – not only me but
 all ...;
For surely everyone who should ... must already
 know —;
That each will answer ... when their name you
 call;
As well your own children ... as the Godless
 foe.

Man would exalt himself to heights that only
 to you are known;
His mind filled with vanity ... he continues to
 pursue ...;
If possible, some would fain sit upon your own
 throne —;
Desiring to be as God ... as the devil declared
 he would do.

Please help us realize we must have forgiveness
 to improve ...;
Believing all who come to you in repentance ...
 you'll not cast out —;
We should feel ourselves a debtor ... from no man
 removed;
Christ died in our stead ... trusting Him will cast
 out doubt.

We're taught not to think of ourselves more highly
 than we ought;
The only good in man is the Spirit of God ... when
 he's born again.
Had man been perfect ... our Salvation wouldn't
 have had to be bought.
Only in obedience and allegiance to Christ, does
 God receive glory from man.

Diligence

Everyone's diligent about ...
Something. What are you diligent
About? Is it a thing you doubt?
No! For to it, focus is lent!

You're "diligent" about "nothing"...
If that's what you do all day long!
Leaving responsibility ...
To others with, "nothing," your song.

Spiritually or materially ...
Diligence works for us the same;
Profit ... promised in all labor;
Without faith ... spirituality, a game.

Without faith, it's impossible ...
To please God: We're told faith's the way;
Leave off faith, work and diligence;
And there'll be nothing but disdain.

We do show our faith by our works:
For without works, our faith is dead!
Living faith's where righteousness lurks;
Diligence needed ... that's Christ led.

There's a Reason

Perhaps, the situation you find yourself in
Is an opportunity to show others right ...
By faith, prove true and do as God would have all men;
Not hide the light, but let His Word shine ever bright.

The world's outlook on life can be dreary and cold;
Not understanding the "why" of things being so:
Faith in the Lord gives strength and will keep the mind whole ...
Causing doubt is the devil's best tool, while man's worst foe.

There must be a purpose in us being where we are,
While eyes focus on Heaven, see what life affords;
Spirit's in harmony with God ... sin cannot mar.
For without faith, it's impossible to please God.

There are always those who will try to help one along;
Adversity brings opportunity to them ...
Living faith in the Lord is needed, to be strong;
The devil brings doubt, and when there's doubt, faith grows dim.

Though heavy low hanging shadows threaten overhead,
If heart is set on the Lord, and He is your guide;
A peace past understanding, when by His Spirit led.
The Lord cares for His own, and with them will abide.

Though astounded when those who presumed to be friends,
In adversity, turned their head and closed their eyes;
Help God sent, from far and near, more than made amends.
Trust not in the flesh, but in God, who is all wise.

Light in the Dark

Such trouble and heartache ... burdened with
    care —;
If it wasn't for the Lord — would be utter
    despair ...
Heavy clouds o'ershadow ... obscuring the
    silver lining;
Yet, faith sees light shining through — the
    dark with silver combining.

The heart so bruised — from things passed
    by —;
Yet, strength ... God gives — through the tears ... and sighs ...
Darkness now — but, the sun is just below the
    horizon;
Faith and trust in the Lord — sees the light
    before it appears — doubt and darkness
    subsiding.
Sunshine does come — though at first flickering —
    Clouds drifting slowly another way ...
Each life has some heartache — brighter days come
    ... not always to stay.
Clouds are an integral part of the tunnel of life
    Also, have their part in the tapestry of day —;
Sunshine's golden threads are woven with dark and
    silver — faith brightening the way.

In times of heartache and trouble ... which every
    life does see —;
Looking beyond self and pity — a flickering beacon
    there'll always be ...
Growing stronger as faith — floods the path of life —
    willing always for God to lead;
Trusting and with thankful heart ... God will always
    supply our need.

Matters Not — Night or Day
(Rondeau)

We go to bed and sleep at night!
Our nerves settle ... once goes the light;
We sleep and snore the whole night through:
If we're so worried ... where's all the fright?
When we're never out of our Lord's sight.

Lacking faith is why we worry ...
Want things our way in a hurry!
From the Lord's perspective ... He sees all;
We go to bed and sleep at night!

Day and night, God's on His throne ...
His strength the same ... when ours is gone:
Day or night ... the Lord we can trust;
By day we feel ALL'S left to us!
Weakness of man, but God is strong;
We go to bed and sleep at night.

Crooked Like a River

Rivers take the path of least resistance;
A characteristic that's common to man ...
Searching an easy way ... bringing chaos,
Like rivers, flowing with lay of land.

Rivers never resist interference ...
Just detour, around obstacles they can;
Some men, rather than face adversity,
Forsake "truth" for whatever's at hand.

A man's life, like a river, grows crooked the same,
Turning from the path, that's narrow and straight;
A desire to dwell in EASE ... only brings blame,
The devil uses money as his bait ...

Love of money's the root of ALL evil ...
God's word, the Bible, tells us this is so:
Seen is mass destruction and upheaval,
The love of money causes many a woe!

When those in a position to make a difference,
Take no heed except to feelings their own;
Example set for posterity ... hence;
God judging ... won't forget what they condone.

Our forefathers with the prophets of old,
Took a stand, with faith in God, to do what's right;
Trusting in Christ, the Savior of their soul:
With recompense of reward shining bright.

Somber Thoughts

Midst the heartache and sorrow
In life, that's common to all;
Minds blot out what the heart knows;
When somber thoughts ... sins recall.

Life viewed from the mountaintop,
More lighthearted thoughts in charge;
Where man's spirit soars nonstop,
And sin doesn't zoom as large.

Somber thoughts search the Spirit ...
Seeking welfare of the soul;
Life's valleys have their purpose,
Enriches life many fold.

Reeds are shaken with the wind,
While the giant Oak's roots reach down:
The Oak, wind tossed, only bends;
After the storm ... reeds not found.

A help to all who know Him,
Our Lord has promised to be;
Works won't be burned as stubble,
When life with God's Word agree.

Somber thoughts bring repentance,
God's Spirit does search the soul;
Condemning what lies between;
And not shining like pure gold.

Low in spirit ... just repent;
Exaltation, yours to know ...
Only then, forgiveness sent:
For God's love can heal all woe.

Waiting

Waiting ... waiting – waiting – for we know
  not what —;
Circumstances may change – and what comes may
  be something we thought not;
God is the only one who sees around the bend
  in life's road ...;
We are just the weary travelers – burdened
  beneath sin's load —;
If we truly desire His help ... we will always
  find;
He not only stays close by—but, His solutions
  are divine.
Trust and obedience are tools not to be cast
  aside —;
Repentance and faith are ever necessary to please
  Him, and with Him to abide.
When waiting for one happening – many others may
  come to pass —;
Leaving the ordering of our life to the One who
  sees all ... our peace can last.

A Ruler

A ruler – is something straight to measure with.
But, without it – to draw a straight line, a myth.
In all things we want done right –
We measure and search the width and girth.
Measuring every nook and cranny;
It must be just right – takes someone brainy!

Are the things of the spirit of man:
Left without a measure in the land?
Nay – this isn't so – God's Word's the plan;
His measure's the same – on mountain or sand!
Where He starts – He looks at the heart!
The Bible – His ruler; we're measured by His Word!

If Any Would Not Work ... Neither Should He Eat!
(2 Th. 3:10)

"If ANY would not work, neither should he eat;"
What's stated in God's word, will always prove right:
This Scripture alone ... much of Welfare defeats.

Many able ... flee work, like a bird in flight:
The Scripture, God's word ... ignored or misconstrued;
To escape work, many try, with all their might.

Part of life's enjoyment comes from work pursued;
With God's word followed and His Spirit to lead,
In tune with the Savior ... allegiance renewed.

With many a dream in life, WORK is the need;
In Creation, God worked six days, then did rest:
Work was meted out to Adam and his seed.

Only Salvation's FREE ... Christ died, gave His best:
By grace, through faith, not of works, or we would fall!
God's Salvation is through Christ ... by which we're blest.

Talents and abilities ... not used ... appall!
Work in life, should not be left forlorn and scorned;
Some eat, that shirk ALL work, yet work is for ALL!

In God's plan for man, work He did not forestall:
"If ANY would not work" ... means ALL who are born!

Death Knocks on Every Door

As death will knock on every door;
Its quota for the day ...
Some go now, others gone before;
Who'll be next? None can say.

As the dead head the funeral march,
Waiting earth's resting place ...
Not know of rain or sun's parch;
Just taking up its space.

When spirit leaves, which was its life;
The body's just a shell ...
Spirit's gone to God who gave it;
At rest or dwells in Hell.

Procession may pass a schoolyard,
Or cattle grazing grain ...
Body in coffin, not on guard;
To enjoy or disdain.

Dead know nothing of what they pass;
In passing to the grave ...
The Bible says they know nothing;
Whether ... they're lost or saved.

It matters not how many years,
Until the Judgment comes ...
The resurrection must come first!
'Till then, the body's dumb.

Why Wait?

One rose
Could mean so much;
If received when it's known;
Not a profusion of roses ...
When dead!

Victory

O' Death!
Where is thy sting?
Grave, where is thy victory?
Death's sting is sin, it's strength, the law;
Christ frees!

Now Known!

A rose
Can be enjoyed,
While one can see and smell;
When heaped upon the coffin you ...
Can't tell!

Be First

We're taught
In the Bible
To do unto others;
As you'd have them do unto you ...
You first!

Enjoy What You Can

Sunset!
A cool evening;
Sitting in porch swing;
Viewing the west's awesome view!
Then rain.

Stop, Look and Listen!

Springtime!
Sun coming up;
Birds singing in the trees,
With song to start the day I need ...
Coffee!

Shhh ...

(Tanka)

A hush, a quiet ...
As death stealthy stalks its prey;
While life's clamor
Rumbles on, never ceasing
Until the end of time.

Ode on Happiness

(Romans 14:22)

Happy is he that does not condemn ...
Himself in that thing which he alloweth;
Constraining fleshly nature so grim,
          To God boweth.

Satisfied with his own lot in life,
If it be exalted or abased ...
Thereby, escaping much of world's strife,
          Through Christ by faith.

Truly seeking God's Will, not his own,
Casting all troubles into greater hands;
Natural man to wrong choices are prone:
          God will set bands.

A sincere desire God's Will be done,
Always smoothes much of life's confusion;
Trust and faith, the ways to overcome ...
          Sight's victory won.

Contentment with peace is happiness,
It's far above rubies ... without price;
Each life Christ can abundantly bless,
          God's sacrifice.

Choices

God created man with the power of choice;
Man is not a stringed puppet with no voice.
The choice of right or wrong lies with each one ...
Responsibility's escaped by none!

We live with results of choices we make;
Seeing our mistake, many times too late,
Other lives affected because of them ...
The Lord will help in what's right ... pray to Him.

We might wish God made the choices for us,
But, that is never the case ... God is just;
He loves and leads us, but we must follow ...
Obeying means a fruitful life ... not one hollow.

When we know Jesus as our own Savior,
God's Sacrifice He gave to save from sin;
When we pray, He gives strength to choose what's right,
In His Will, He gives power with His great might.

Heart to Heart

Man's heart fails from what is seen,
Coming to the whole earth;
Christ came, lost souls to redeem,
All are sinners by birth.

Born into sin by Adam's fall,
Forgiveness brings its peace;
Convictions with faith do call.
And repentance, sin's release.

Peace above understanding,
Only felt in the heart;
Is what Salvation will bring,
It is free; works not part.

Circumstances won't hinder,
The peace Christ brings within,
In the world, turmoil does reign ...
With God's rest, hearts will mend.

All Things . . .

At times, things come into our lives,
We can't figure or understand why.
Trust the Lord and do our best is wise.

If certain things hadn't come about;
And we'd chosen another path in life,
We wouldn't be where we are, no doubt.

It's enough that God is all-knowing.
Nothing comes into our lives without His permission.
There's a Scripture: Romans 8:28 – with need of quoting.

"All things work together for good –
To them that love God, to them who are –
The called according to His purpose."

Next time you feel such frustration;
Refer to the Scripture in the verse above.
Do you love God? – Ask yourself the question!

If we would concentrate on doing our job,
Not always try to run God's business.
Then we would certainly be separated from the mob!

A Tribute to Loving Dads

Men marry, wanting a home and children;
Working long hours, weary to the bone,
With all their heart, giving time and love:
To the young children, God gave on loan.

Never can a woman be a true success,
To the neglect of home, as it were ...
To fulfill own desires, that's the test;
Do God and family come first with her?

A selfish "mother" is always a failure;
It matters not at all what she does ...
Her heart can't be right with God nor pure,
When neglect of children IS and WAS.

When a woman cares nothing for her own,
In sickness, leaving all care to dad ...
No surprise ... when such are left alone;
Being a, "mother" takes work ... it is no fad.

Two loving parents for a child's so good!
Many times a dad must take up the slack,
When a selfish mother just doesn't care,
If not for the dad, a child would lack.

Charity should always begin at home,
Everyone has often heard it said ...
If social services ... one condones,
Then compassion, love ... with home should wed.

In Judgment, parents will give account;
For love and care given little ones;
It's very sad, but many times, true ...
Some homes ... dad is dad, and mother, too.

Greatest job any woman can have,
Is caring for and raising a family;
Where her children rise up to bless her,
For teaching God's Salvation is free.

For all dads who love with all their heart;
With God's help, doing the best they can:
While seeing unconcern on mate's part,
A situation that befalls many a man.

Love and gratitude from children's due –
Those dads, who love, care and work so hard;
Teaching you right ... providing for you ...
Honor him ... with the highest regard.

The Past

Looking down memory lane where I have passed:
Standing on time's incline, thoughts looking back,
Much escaped the light and dark shadows cast ...
Path lies straighter now travel isn't lacked.
With much obscured ... protection it can be;
Eyes not deterred from goal as summit seized;
Obstacles not deemed or as none to see ...
Meandering through as wind the leaves do tease.
Decisions alter many a life's path ...
Trust in the Lord overcomes much danger:
Faith sails unhampered o'er boulders and ravines;
Man's born to trouble and never a stranger.
Faith sees the best route, is letting God lead;
With Him providing as He sees the need!

Easter Brings Hope

Easter is known as Christ's resurrection:
It is befitting, it comes in the spring;
A time for renewal that eyes cannot shun,
Earth's plants start to green ... birds begin to sing.

For man's sin, our Savior was crucified;
He died as our substitute on the Cross ...
While by grace, through faith, we are justified,
Repentance brings forgiveness to the lost.

Our Savior lay in the grave for three days;
At Christ's resurrection ... God's plan was done:
The devil through man, devised many ways ...
But, God for Salvation ... has only one.

If Salvation could come another way,
God sent His Son, Jesus, to die in vain;
Jesus died on the Cross, our sin to pay,
God so loved the world ... Jesus bore the pain.

When Easter comes to mind ... think Christ instead;
The sacrifice He made for you and me,
Was resurrected after He was dead ...
God's plan for Salvation is all there be!

Easter and Springtime

Christ's resurrection ... Easter celebrates;
How befitting it comes in the springtime,
For it's springtime when all nature awakens;
God's universe, in tune, His plan to rhyme,

And Christ was the firstfruits of them that slept.
Christ died to save lost souls, after man's fall;
Man's first estate he did not keep, by choice ...
ALL can be saved, who on Christ's name, will call.

Salvation's a free gift ... can never be bought:
God gave His only Son; Christ gave His life;
Law of sin ... Christ's resurrection defied ...
Christ ... The ONLY WAY ... the devil's is rife.

Winter snow melts under the sun's warm gleam;
Spring flowers come forth midst decayed debris;
Soon crocus, jonquils, tulips are seen ...
Christ came forth from the grave, as God decreed.

Easter celebrates Christ's resurrection ...
Springtime brings renewed life, nature's bequeath;
Beauties of nature and Salvation's free ...
Christ triumphed o'er sin ... came forth from beneath.

A Different Perspective

Each year Christmas comes, ... Christmas goes,
Still remembered is "Sharon's Rose;"
Christ came to earth so long ago ...
God's promised Savior we all know.

After the tree is taken down,
And gifts left in diminished mound –
There's peace that comes from knowing Christ;
For Salvation, He paid God's price.

The merchandising of Christmas ...
An excuse for some to get gain;
The true meaning of it will bring
Joy to the heart ... while angels sing.

While you wait for one day each year
There are three hundred sixty-four that are still dear ...
Christ will never leave or forsake;
When He as Savior you do take.

Christmas in the Air

Wind blowing, ground carpeted in white ...
    snowflakes falling,
        the scent of pine and cedar fill the air;
Icicles glistening like diamonds on the evergreens and on trees
    which were bare —;
Christmas soon to be here ... people with faces that glow and eyes
    shining like stars ... running here and there;
Street crowded with children and adults ... last minute shoppers ...
    just must dare.

We all look forward to Christmas ... our children and families
    have been planning to come since early fall ...;
Grandchildren can hardly wait to get here ... each time on
phone
    they call —;
Looking forward to Christmas with music and singing, games, gifts,
    a feast of wonderful food ... giant tree in the hall;
Home for Christmas ... thankfulness with laughter, good cheer ...
    prayer fills the hearts of one and all.

Christmas is the time for family to be together ... blessings ...
    with fellowship that lasts ...;
Thinking back over all the good times when our children were small
    ... and of Christmases past —;
Remembering when everyone was younger ... some have
already gone
    to be with the Lord ... looking back over years that are vast;
It seems just a short while ... when our children were the age of
    their children ... years have passed so fast.

Many things we enjoy in celebrating as a family, but the true
    meaning of Christmas ... everyone knows ...;
Always the young are taught the truth of Jesus' birth ... recorded
    for all in Luke, Chapter 2 ... as the Bible story goes;
Love for the Lord, and love for each other – with a good visit and
    thankful hearts ... help with life's woes —;
Appreciation for blessings and God's care ... increases as one
    older grows.

All Year Long

Christmas is celebrated as the birth of Christ,
It's over two thousand years since the manger scene;
Seeking the Christ-Child, to bring about His demise ...
The devil used King Herod ... who was vicious and mean.

Christ, the Savior of the world, is the heart's true light,
It's by grace through faith that comes everlasting life ...
The Star of Bethlehem shown to shepherds that night;
Bringing peace and goodwill to a world of sinful strife.

The Spirit of Christmas can live in every heart,
Though Christmas decorations are no longer seen ...
When Christ dwells within a heart, His Spirit works its part;
For by grace through faith, not works, man's soul is redeemed.

The Spirit of Christmas endures sorrow and pain ...
It can survive midst trouble, heartache and sorrow;
After "Twelve Days of Christmas," Spirit doesn't wane,
But, all year long, Christ makes the Christmas spirit glow.

The essence of Christmas is to saving the soul;
For that purpose, Jesus in the manger was born.
The Little Babe, the Wise Men, did seek and behold!
He lived, died on the cross, to save souls, few did mourn.

Christ was resurrected, after paying the cost ...
Christmas should be a reminder ... lost souls need be won;
God so loved the world, He sent Christ, to save the lost:
The true meaning of Christmas is ... faith in God's Son.

Christmas Means More Than Shopping and Spice

It's almost Christmas again!
Many things must need be done.
The air is brisk and chilly,
Clouds play at hiding the sun.

Shopping is not yet finished ...
Reviewing names ... missing none;
At each shop, list diminished,
All the shopping is such fun!

With baking ... air reeks of spice,
Cookies, pies, and cakes – all have a share;
Each one finished seems so nice,
New recipes tried with care.

Is this what Christmas is about???
Whole world knows the answer's ... "NO!"
"Christmas" ... the birth of Jesus ...
Date celebrated as so!

Midst hurrying to and fro ...
Take some time to think and pray;
Thank God for His Gift of Love:
His Son, who in a manger lay.

Enjoy Christmas with loved ones ...
Reflect on our Savior's love;
How He died on Calvary's cross,
Sent to us from God above.

Christmas ... a Season for giving,
The best gift ... give Christ your heart;
A more abundant life living ...
When saved ... does True Life then start!!!

Do You Worship the Lord, or the Christmas Tree?

(Jeremiah 10:1-7)

For the customs of the people are vain,
Out of the forest one cutteth a tree ...
By the hands of the workman with the axe,
This describes "Christendom" at Christmastime.

They deck the tree with silver and with gold,
Upright as the palm tree, but it speaks not,
They must be borne because they cannot go,
Fastened with nails and hammers, it does hold.

Do not fear trees ... evil they cannot do!
And neither is it in them to do good,
We're not to learn the way of the heathen,
Nor be dismayed at the signs of Heaven.

We're told, the heathen are dismayed at them,
As there is none like unto thee, O Lord,
Thou art great, and thy name is great in might,
Who would not fear thee, O King of Nations?

World should say, ... "Oh, Lord and King we worship!"
And not, "Oh, tree, oh, tree, oh, Christmas tree,"
We all should celebrate our Savior's birth,
With true worship ... the way it ought to be.

A Gift of Love

Christmas will be here soon;
We see signs everywhere ...
Tinsel shines in the gloom,
Music heard here and there.

Shoppers laden with gifts,
Trudging the icy streets ...
Snowfall piling in drifts;
Cheerfulness ... can't defeat.

Cheeks are rosy with cold,
Like Rudolph ... noses red;
Packages hard to hold ...
As in snow, shoppers tread.

Trees hold many bright lights,
Houses light up the dark ...
"Stars" beam on lawns once green;
Carolers fill each park.

Christ's birth we celebrate:
But, gifts we give to men ...
Twenty-fifth is the date;
Is this the "birthday" trend?

All He asks is our heart,
By faith and trust in Him:
And ... man's works have no part;
Salvation's gift won't dim!

Christ was born in a manger;
He died to save lost souls ...
He arose so that we could live;
King of Kings ... ALL behold!!!

Father's Day
(Triolet)

It's "Father's Day" again ... this year:
Love ... in hustle and bustle, is seen ...
It's a day to families that's dear!
It's "Father's Day" again ... this year:
Visits, calls, cards; from far and near;
Gifts and feast fit for a king;
It's "Father's Day" again ... this year:
Love ... in hustle and bustle, is seen.

When You Have Children of Your Own
(Triolet)

You never knew such love 'till now;
When you have children of your own:
Times on your knees to God you bow!
You never knew such love 'till now;
For such love you didn't allow ...
Then children of your flesh and bone!
You never knew such love 'till now;
When you have children of your own.

Maybe and Maybe Not!
(Cinquain)

That child!
Needs correction ...
Should never be let go!
Must be strict! I will be ... when I
Have some.

Springtime
(Cinquain)

Test day ...
Some are barely
Awake, others just here,
Resting head on desk ... in between
Answers.

Mother's Day
(Triolet)

Mother's Day, one day must suffice ...
What of the three hundred sixty-four?
One day ... everyone's so very nice ...
Mother's Day, one day must suffice;
If spoiled, what's needed done might think twice!
And all things mothers do, might become a chore.
Mother's Day, one day must suffice:
What of the three hundred sixty-four?

You're Mine!

You are my Valentine!
And have been for so long;
Many years gone behind ...
"Cupid's" bow proved so strong.

Arrow made two hearts one,
No longer ... separate ...
Perfect aim without a gun,
Where two hearts integrate.

I love you, "Valentine ..."
I do with all my heart.
You have to say you were mine,
When joined by "Cupid's" dart!

For: Carl
With Love

Valentine's Day?
Everyday!

Valentine's Day is the perfect day – with reason to say,
    "I love you ..."
But, why wait so long ... someone more interested may
    come along –;
Then, perhaps you'll always wonder – why you wait around
    the way you do;
In secret, you truly loved – for so very long ... now your
    heart is filled with sadness instead – of song.

Three hundred sixty-five days a year – letting years
    go by ...;
Then, on Valentine's Day ... Cupid and arrow on card
    is sent;
With all the time gone by ... the disquiet of heart living
    the lie –;
For each time, when thinking of you ... heart feeling Cupid's
    arrow – for not mended – the rent.

Wasted time ... is never brought back – to be
    lent –;
Loving to all hearts should be, not a rarity – but, an
    integral part;
Be it Valentine's Day – when all type cards, with loving
    words are sent;
Or Sunday, Monday, Tuesday, Wednesday, Thursday, Friday,
    Saturday – all year ... giving our heart!

An Irish Valentine

My Irish heritage ... for this I'm ever –
    thankful —;
There's a depth of heart – home and love are
    so much a part;
It matters not – "if you're Irish ..." there's nothing –
    work or play ... that's dull ...
That spark that's always an integral part ... of the
    heart – is the start.

Valentine's Day ... with the Irish is an everyday
    affair ...
Through hardships monumental ... famine and drought –
    having to leave Emerald Isle —;
Still, what was deep set in brave loving hearts ...
    coming to a new country – to dare;
A little bit of Ireland was brought with each one –
    in laughter and smiling eyes from there.

Appreciation of family and friends – love of God –
    runs strong – defeating despair —;
Being able to make even work fun ... is an ability
    not many inherit;
A song in the heart – knowing difficulties are
    surmountable – with faith in God is not so rare ...
Mostly you think one of Irish lineage – even though missing
    the language lilt, — a Valentine without a care.

For: My four children

Straight Shooter
(Triolet)

If Cupid's bow does shoot a straight line,
Love's arrow never goes awry ...
Piercing two hearts ... true love to twine;
If Cupid's bow does shoot a straight line,
A ricocheted dart many hearts find:
For heartache, true love will defy;
If Cupid's bow does shoot a straight line,
Love's arrow never goes awry ...

Where's the Stuff?
(Triolet)

Valentine's Day ... celebrates love,
One day a year just isn't enough!
Many cards, candy, flowers sent ...
Valentine's Day ... celebrates love,
All know love is a many splendored thing:
The rest of the year ... where's the "stuff?"
Valentine's Day ... celebrates love,
One day a year just isn't enough!

Sunrise in Summer

As the sun comes up in the strength of the morning;
Delicate blooms and grass still glisten with dew.
Butterflies and bees, the flowers adorning.
Busy little hummingbirds are quite a few.
Not outdone by all goings on – just joining.
Since gathering their food – energy renewed!

Air filled with sweet melodious songs;
Over the grass and clover-filled meadow,
Birds twittering and singing as they hop along.
Searching all around for the "early bird" – worms.
It's as if they heard the "breakfast gong!"
Food for themselves and tiny little ones.

Cattle grazing under the Green Bay Tree;
The calves close by, saying, "Moo" ... and gamboling about.
Kicking playfully – such antics – so free!
Also a mother and colt, without a doubt,
Are alert for any danger they might see,
Though tame – going for water another route!

The fresh morning air so exhilarating!
Bright summer sun just lighting the east.
A huge ball of fire, flowing, it seems – waiting —.
Exploding all of a sudden with brightness – energy released.
With the sun moving above the earth's rim, darkness relieving;
God in His wisdom – gave such light – with beauty increased.

Everything Going Wrong
(Triolet)

When you think everything is going wrong,
And begin to feel sorry for yourself ...
If you really look, you'll know before long;
When you think everything is going wrong,
Through more troubles than you, many have gone;
There's no one in this world from troubles left;
When you think everything is going wrong,
And begin to feel sorry for yourself.

Beauty Plus

Big blue eyes, flawless skin and curly hair,
Such an intelligent, beautiful little girl;
Always busy – and with courage to spare,
In spite of a world of difficulties hurled;
Struggling on no matter how she would fare.
From the start, this little girl 'round my heart was curled.

Many hours – child's games, we played together,
What she excelled at was games of skill;
When staying inside because of the weather;
She accomplished much because of strong will.
Others might their wits fail to gather;
But, always with her, discouragement was nil!

When upset with me, I still remember …
Her pushing her doll buggy filled with dolls;
Giving them back – loving them so, didn't matter.
It never was long until down the hall, …
Skipping along – buggy and dolls she would gather.
Quiet once again, in the dollhouse walls.

She always excelled in all at school.
From the start – to college finished;
Give of your best, was always her rule.
In all things in life, pettiness banished;
Honesty, goodness, mercy – faith in God, her tool.
Studying, writing, always learning – reaching for knowledge,
    as one famished.

Literary Sidewinders

In writing ... the paramount desire should be –
    to be understood ...
If no one is able to decipher or unravel ...
    why take the time to write?
Much time is spent in discussion – it means this –
    it means that – when understand they would ...
Why the discussion – when the writer perhaps said –
    just what he would – not vague at all – yet a
    continual, "literary fight."

The Apostle Paul said he would rather speak five
    words – able to teach others, than ten thousand words –
otherwise.
If we have something to write about – a lesson all
    should learn ...
Why play at intelligence ... only to improvise – while
    for the meaning ... all just surmise!
The truth is permanent ... never varied – not as a
    pendulum swinging in time to turn.

Whatever type writing ... content should head the list ...
    with understanding coming first –;
Not just the rhyming of poetry – and using of style –
    all words have meaning – important in their use;
No one should be left in doubt or guessing ... not
    being overly terse ...
Some writing can be compared to the "sidewinder,"
    so many twists and turns – making obscure what's obtuse.

Spring

The first of spring is so exciting!
Birds singing, buds growing on trees;
Things appearing which have been hiding;
The first of spring is so exciting!
Flowers, their time have been abiding;
Grass and trees turning green by degrees;
The first of spring is so exciting!
Birds singing, buds growing on trees.

Just Listen

I love listening to the soft rain;
Another of nature's sounds ...
As small animals scurry in the lane;
I love listening to the soft rain;
Laughing children running for shelter;
Making their way across the grounds,
I love listening to the soft rain;
Another of nature's sounds.

Lilac Flowers
(Triolet)

Lilacs are beautiful flowers.
Their fragrance so very nice.
Lilacs bloom with spring showers.
Lilacs are beautiful flowers.
Queenly flowers to adorn bowers,
Fragile beauty without price.
Lilacs are beautiful flowers.
Their fragrance so very nice.

Butterflies
(Triolet)

Butterflies of gossamer web.
Fragile little rainbows with wings,
As sunlight to prisms are wed,
Butterflies of gossamer web,
From flower to flower they are led,
Colorful designs from spots to fringe.
Butterflies of gossamer web,
Fragile little rainbows with wings.

To Each His Own

All trees in their winter dress;
Icicles glistening ... through snow ...
In spring, they're dressed in so much less;
Before the buds can grow.

Ice and snow ... tree's hair dressed to go;
Sequined skirt at the base ...
Bird barrettes do show ... as wind blows;
Diamonds hold ... all in place.

Each season has its own beauty;
The Lord does give great change ...
Unsurpassed artwork ... is all free;
While God does rearrange.

A Great God and Loving Savior;
Gives beauty with His care ...
We need ask and seek His favor;
Without which ... life is bare.

In winter, enjoy what you can;
When springtime ... do the same...
Summertime fun covers the land;
Fall's beauty ... like a flame.

Four seasons from which you can choose;
Whichever you like best ...
Beauty ... the seasons never lose;
Choose one, but like the rest.

Tanka

The birds
Flying through the air
So free ...
While man's Spirit soars
Above the moon and stars.

Tanka

As the rose
Parades its beauty,
For awhile ...
Youth's bloom will fade;
Aging stalks until death.

Tanka

Springtime!
Soon summer is here;
Autumn leaves fall ...
Cold of winter at hand:
Life is like four seasons.

Tanka

Though our sins
Be known as scarlet;
Christ in forgiveness,
Makes them, white as snow:
Though crimson, they'll be as wool.

Never Seen

The wind
Is felt, not seen,
Though effects can be known;
In hurricanes, tornadoes and ...
Cyclones.

For All

He's mine!
He can be yours;
Christ died to set us free;
By grace through faith we are saved ... it's
Your choice.

Everything For Me!

So sad!
Think of others,
Selfishness never pays!
Others have needs the same as you ...
Their right.

Put God First

Values
With truth as base,
Are learned from the Bible;
We read what God would have us do ...
Love Him.

Too Late

Show now
While there's still time;
Love you have for others ...
Don't wait until from earth they've gone;
Then cry!

My Little Shadow

Shadow's beside me, I can see,
She's my little Schipperke friend;
And from the start, she has been;
Always first, she runs to me.

I don't own her, she owns me!
Shadow makes known, I'm her own;
She's happy when I get home;
She's my little Schipperke.

She's my Shadow I adore,
Dressed up or coming from work;
Her feelings are never hurt;
Always meets me at the door.

Whether my hair's combed or not;
And makeup is on my face;
If Shadow cares ... there's no trace;
I don't think she cares one jot!

Continued

Shadow is always the same,
Just waiting to hear her name.
When I'm sick or feeling bad,
She wags her tail so I won't be sad.

If only I can be there,
She's happy with little attention;
Relieves much of life's tension;
Shadow and I are a pair.

Shadow's manners are very good;
She's polite, never encroaches;
Hasn't been to obedience school,
But, first in line, she'd have stood!

Shadow's beside me, I can see,
She's my little Schipperke friend;
And from the start, she has been;
Since I'm first, she comes to me!

Sestina

Maxine's logical, mathematical mind made this type of poetic form one of her favorites. The sestina has six stanzas of six lines each in which the first stanza's line end words recur at the end of all the other lines. The writer thinks of six simple words upon which to build a story, according to this prescribed form. Maxine makes it look easy and fun.

A heavy overcast covers the summer sky,
Rain will soon descend by the looks of the clouds;
The animals and fowls are headed for the barn,
The billy goat is hiding his head, waving his beard.
Such wind! With the noise of the low flying airplane;
Also, sounds like a train, but could be a tornado.

Can't tell just yet if it's high winds or a tornado;
Though there'd be debris twirling through the sky.
Such a deafening roar, seems more than an airplane.
The sky is rolling with dark black clouds ...
As the billy goat's face is covered by his beard;
While ahead of other animals he runs for the barn.

The wind is blowing the tin on roof of the barn,
Much damage will be done whether just wind or tornado.
The billy goat may lose his beard!
Before the wind dies down and clears the sky;
Such a haze of greenish, yellow, black clouds;
Danger in some winds, even for an airplane.

Continued

With strong winds, birds can fly high as an airplane;
While the winds twist the tin on the top of the barn.
The night comes so early because of the dark clouds,
With everyone running for shelter, thinking it's a tornado.
Not a bit of sun can be seen in afternoon sky ...
The billy goat getting into the barn saved his beard!

Billy would have been perturbed to lose his beard;
He's even scared of the sound of an airplane –
As it flies low overhead in the sky ...
He always makes his way fast to the barn;
Thinking he's in for another tornado!
As he shakes his head looking up at the clouds.

For anyone, it can be scary just looking at the clouds;
Too many scares, hair may turn white, so may Billy's beard!
No one wants to think they're in for a tornado ...
He'd rather it be a formation of many an airplane;
Even though he runs fast as he can to the barn;
Looking up to see what there may be in the sky.

The whole sky is covered in dark clouds;
Animals are all in the barn, with Billy shaking his beard;
Listening to see if it's an airplane or another tornado.

The Mouse

The mouse is so very small,
Goes anyplace, slips under doors,
Nibbles its way ... not by force,
Scampers out, while the house snores.

Up one wall, down the other,
Little field mouse moves about,
In an instant changes route,
Darting here and there, hiding.

Traps are set, poison put out,
Still, they thrive on what they find,
A few crumbs is all it takes,
Always mice! Just be resigned!

Where there are people there'll be mice,
Whether in barn or castle ...
They make their way, take their time,
Instead of a few – a passel!

Continued

Lots of damage, a mouse can do!
Over time, it shreds and tears,
Though timid it seems, is so fleet,
Where one is seen ... there are pairs!

A mouse must have a sense of humor!
Often lets himself be seen ...
In a room full of people,
With his beady eyes agleam!

Upon table, women jump!
Screaming, screeching hysterically,
Guess they're more familiar with rats!
He's outnumbered numerically!

The mouse is so very small,
Goes anyplace, slips under doors,
Nibbles its way ... not by force,
Scampers out, while the rat snores!

They're Back!

The little lizards we see dart about,
Could be dinosaurs we thought were extinct.

The environment could have made them like dwarves;
So much pollution, they just couldn't grow.

Could the earth's pollution have played a part?
It seems the environmentalists should know!

Would "Garden Grow" help until we could check?
That way a committee would have time to reflect.

Do you think lizards could be in disguise?
Yes, they do look the same ... just small in size.

Has this come up for discussion before?
Doubtful ... or we would have heard from Al Gore!

Is there something we can do about it?
Ask help of the FED ... it will take a bit.

What about all the committee's red tape?
We'll use " Garden Grow" before it's too late.

Why haven't the environmentalists checked this?
There are too many spotted owls on their list.

Do you know how many lizards there are?
No dinosaur size, or the whole earth they'll mar.

The Cabbage Patch

Early in the year, cabbage plants appear ...
Time to put them out ... so the roots can sprout;
When the plants do good – a delight to see —;
Big cabbage heads ... and many there'll be.
The rabbits hop right up to the thriving cabbage patch;
Under the fence – makes no difference if gate has a latch.

Each morning you'll see pieces of leaves about ...
Where rabbits have nibbled ... they leave no doubt;
Nibbling from one cabbage to the other and on to the next;
Tasting all leaves ... as if they were vexed ...
As if one cabbage might taste better than the other —;
Wanting to make sure ... still hopping further.

Some cabbage heads ... grow so very large ...
If having a chance to grow ... from the nibbling barrage;
No plant for food in looks ... more to the eye appealing;
Looking like a big cabbage rose ... but deceiving ...
The "Cabbage Patch Doll" we've all seen ...
So ugly to look at ... the cabbage heads do demean.

A Vow is a Vow is a Vow!
(Triolet)

The marriage vow ... "Until death do us part,"
Can mean hours, days, weeks, months or many years!
Vows should come from the very depths of heart.
The marriage vow ... "Until death do us part,"
Is witnessed by God, as the home they start:
Knowing Christ as Savior, calms through all fears;
The marriage vow ... "Until death do us part,"
Can mean hours, days, weeks, months, or many years!

Be Careful What You Vow!
(Cinquain)

The vow ...
"Until death do
Us part ..." needs come from heart:
Time may be long ... 'till comes the Grim
Reaper!

Forgotten
(Limerick)

Leaving the place with spouse laid to rest,
Tear-filled eyes, for living, no zest;
Then is seen "Cupid's" bow —
Forgotten, sorrow and all woe,
So soon made ready for another nest!

Unusual

The nighttime was made for sleeping;
Off with shoes when going to bed!
With slumber's "zzz's" the mind sweeping,
When clothes are changed, to rest the head.

The morning of A.C.T. Test!
Finds many eyes drooping with sleep;
Removing shoes to do their best??
Heard remarked ... this would make scores leap!

Fifteen or twenty pairs in a row;
Owners await signal to write ...
Shoes all sizes ... both high and low,
Improve test score? ... They say, "That's right!"

Time runs out with the timer's "ding;"
There's such a start midst the "sleepy" group,
Eyes open wide ... seems dreams take wing;
Test in hand, but "out of the loop."

There's such a scramble at end of test,
Each determined to find his shoe ...
Not finding their own ... did their best!
One of a kind ... there were quite a few!

An April Fools' Essay!

April fools' ... they forgot!
Sometimes, fun voids tension,
Date remembered or not ...
Not one did dare mention!

A.C.T. Test today ...
The first one of springtime!
Energy held at bay,
And spring fever combine.

Test giver makes it fun ...
While making sure it's right;
Settled for test ... fun done!
Relaxed ... scores reach new height.

Proverbs states ... "A merry heart
Doeth good ... like a medicine;"
Attitude plays a great part,
Life can be right ... and fun!

Though there's much noise to start ...
Test time they settle down;
Doing best on each part ...
More scholarships are found.

Continued

Springtime it's ... spring fever;
Winter ... it is so cold ...
Fall ... ball games here and there,
And summer's test, looms bold.

"No good time to take a test,"
... Some are overheard say;
With God's help, do your best,
Many a test down life's way.

When Christ is Lord of a life,
No test is faced alone.
He's there midst strife;
But, sin ... never condones.

After timed test was through,
The test giver just said;
"There'll be an essay, too ..."
They moaned and shook their heads.

Leaving soon ... all thoughts dead,
Then said ... "April Fools'!"

Greenbrier High School
(For those testing in the theatre)
Maxine helped proctor the American
College Testing (ACT) for ten years.

Keepsake
(Triolet)

It was given as a keepsake,
    Just a small gift,
Said it was a fake,
It was given as a keepsake,
Found it was no fake, what I did take
    I was not to be miffed,
It was given as a keepsake,
    Just a small gift.

A Cutting
(Triolet)

A cutting is what it was,
    A piece from a yellow rose,
It has grown to what it is,
A cutting is what it was,
A beautiful bush, it's his.
    He'll give you a cutting, I suppose.
A cutting is what it was,
    A piece from a yellow rose.

Just Take Time to Remember

He came when he had a three-day pass;
But, since he was stationed so far away,
The time taken in travel was vast ...
Still, we both looked forward to that day.

In spring, summer, fall or winter's ice,
When time for his pass, he would leave fast;
Heading for those Oklahoma Hills ...
Time he got there his "pass" almost past.

Such little time, it did seem quite sad,
Coming so far ... with his stay so short;
Busy with school, but, to see him, glad;
Time fleeting, with the clock, time's cohort.

When out of the Air Force, we married:
Soon to be fifty-three years ago ...
Our love, with the Lord's help has carried
Us through hardships ... blessings to bestow.

When we were young, God called him to preach,
The highest calling to man, in life ...
Our home was blessed with children to teach;
God blessed me, too, being a preacher's wife.

We'll just take the time to remember:
If ever's the time we should forget ...
Experience the longing, as it were;
The nostalgia ... of when we first met!

For Carl,
With Love

Sweetheart, Another Anniversary

It's our Anniversary ...
You know – we've had quite a few,
Few days and full of trouble;
God's promise to me and you.

Another promise He's made ...
He'll never leave or forsake;
A very present help in
Trouble, is His promise, too.

So much to be thankful for ...
Good times there's been, through the bad,
And for richer or poorer ...
Through sickness and health, to add.

Whatever the years may bring ...
In our hearts, God's love abides;
Salvation removes death's sting,
Christ's blood every sin doth hide.

Life's triumphs and failures are rife ...
Our days with strife are filled,
Our children accepted Christ,
We taught them about God's will.

Sweetheart, in that we failed not,
They're saved for eternity; not many's lot.
Hell will be so very hot,
In Heaven, our home will be.

Not through any works we've done ...
By grace through faith we are saved,
For Christ is the only one,
All others are so depraved!

Anniversary!
(Triolet)

It's our fifty-second Anniversary!
Our daughter sent us out to eat to celebrate;
Eyes dim, ears dull ... hard to tell when others greet;
It's our fifty-second Anniversary!
He begged own pardon ... I admired my own dress;
Wall of mirrors confused my mate and me,
It's our fifty-second Anniversary!
Our daughter sent us out to eat to celebrate.

God's Man
(Triolet)

He's a preacher, who loves to preach!
Since God called him over sixty years ago!
He's continued, his call not to breach,
He's a preacher who loves to preach!
Lost souls, to accept Christ, he does beseech,
To save the lost, rescue from the foe,
He's a preacher who loves to preach!
Since God called him over sixty years ago!

Time Change
(Tanka)

Girl or boy,
Many rejoice with parents;
Meticulous ...
Night feedings last so long;
School age before you know it!

True Love
(Triolet)

True love not contingent on circumstance:
It twines true hearts like tendrils of ivy!
True love desires other's life to enhance;
True love not contingent on circumstance:
Can flourish in obscure shack or elegance;
In poverty or wealth ... ill health or lively;
True love not contingent on circumstance:
It twines two hearts like tendrils of ivy!

Nostalgia

Nostalgia is just what it seems,
Handpicked memories, over time:
The ones clasped tight, are what we dream;
What's unpleasant, put out of mind.

Can be compared to a baby's birth;
After pain and travail's over ...
Love for the newborn ... joy and mirth,
All pain forgotten, as it were.

The mind remains a wonderful thing:
To its advantage ... it defends ...
If comfort's needful ... that it brings,
Hides away hurts, if peace they bend;

Giving the spirit a chance to heal;
As a man thinketh in his heart so ...
Is he ... a lapsing of time, pain steals:
A merry heart doeth good like medicine.

Nostalgia reaches back in years,
Desired memories it gathers ...
With a cause of sorrow and pain feared
   ... Or all would be ... as, "mad hatters!"

Memory Lane
(Quatrain)

As I contemplate the past,
To my memory much is fast:
More forgotten than I know,
On down memory lane I go.

Years have passed in thinking back;
Tracks of time the lane does pack:
Hardships seem to lose much awe;
Part of nature's aging law.

Blessings count more than before,
Pleasures just outside the door;
Life is gone ... time the master:
Memory lane moves on faster.

Memory cache ... ever condone,
Memories stored, never alone;
Just a few steps down the lane,
So much joy! Outweighs the pain.

The Lord's been with me from my youth;
Faith increased, is based on truth:
Knowing how He's brought me through;
Memories unfold ... not a few!

The Lilac

Lilacs are beautiful flowers,
Their fragrance so very nice.
Colors ... white, purple and red,
Fragile beauty knows no price.

Lilacs are an old known flower,
Generations past have enjoyed,
Adorning, enchanting, perfuming bowers,
Profusion — covering a void.

Lilacs can be used in food,
Their fragrance not a hindrance,
A lilac bush makes a view,
Spreading along wall or fence.

Lilacs are beautiful in groups,
Tiny flowers, covering a spike,
They appear to be one flower
Colors of purple, red or white.

My Birthday

My birthday ... is going to be here – is coming right
    away —;
After having so many ... impulse is to ... just have them
    stay!
But, as each year comes ... and birthday date comes skipping
    along ...
Thanks should be given to God – for the giving of time,
    not using it wrong.

The "cake" and "feast" are quite fancy ... besides the
    gifts which means —;
Someone took a lot of time to bake and cook something
    nice for me ...
There'll be presents ... such a variety ... easily explained ...
    by individual choices driven.
Each having his own idea ... as to what gift should be
    given.

Continued

It's my birthday ... yet, everyone there gets a gift – oh,
   just a little present ...
A gift is given to those who are at the party ... honoring
   me with their presence.
So ... "Happy birthday," to me ... perhaps many more I'll
   be privileged to see ...
With loved ones gathered around me ... enjoying them every-
   one – until my time on earth is done.

We all know ... our lives are temporal ... or should – at
   least.
The Bible tells us this life is as a vapor ... soon we
   all are of the deceased.
The soul will live forever ... and if Heaven ... is our
   goal —;
Christ must live in our heart ... the integral part ... for
   the Salvation of our soul.
We should rejoice in the time – with family we
   have left —;
Witnessing as we ought, perhaps there'll be another
   saved ... not knowing when with time we'll be bereft;
Happy birthday to me – happy birthday to myself ... and
   many happy returns ...
The longer permitted to live ... the more birthdays God
   gives ... the more we should trust Him and learn.

Another Year Older

Another birthday ... another year ...
Seems each time ... everything's more dear;
From each family member – so good to hear –;
With all their love and good wishes – sincere;
Thanking everyone far away or near ...
For His loving care – thanking God – shedding a tear;

Bringing us through many things – many fears;
With faith in God and waiting for Christ to appear;
For whatever birthdays – there are left to bear;
Trusting our Lord to forgive all sin in arrears;
In letting Him lead – our lives He will repair;
Though the devil vies for our lives – our souls, he won't dare.

January Twenty-Ninth

It's January twenty-ninth,
An important date to me;
For me, the year's starting time:
It's January twenty-ninth;
As my birthdays fall behind,
Brighter do God's blessings gleam;
It's January twenty-ninth,
An important date to me.

Barefoot Boy Turned Barefoot Man

Barefoot boy turned barefoot man ...
Still goes barefoot, when he can;
He loves to walk the hills and streams;
All this his ... to him it seems.
In the hills, he hunts wild game;
When the redbuds are in flame;
Fishing, in the creek he stands,
Rod held sturdily, in his hands;
His catch safely, on the line;
To him, they looked mighty fine.
After awhile he wades to shore;
Rocks are hot, his feet are sore.
It's a long way, to trudge home;
Most all day he has been gone;
As he walks, he'll eat his lunch,
Just an apple he did crunch!
Busy fishing the whole time ...
Missed his lunch, but didn't mind.
As he walks ... the sun does set,
Darkness comes, he does not fret;
Blindfolded he'd win a prize ...
Knowing ... since he was no size –
Those who know him, they would say;
Never would he lose his way!

Continued

Barefoot boy turned barefoot man,
Growing up ... don't bare feet ban;
Moon and stars show in the night,
Not a thing his life to blight;
It's his holiday to choose ...
Zest for living, he won't lose.
City folk lose out on much ...
Feet all cramped with shoes and such.
Don't give up on fun in life –
If you ever take a wife ...
Keep the freedom that you had,
When you were a barefoot lad.
All God made was good and true,
And He made it just for you!
Sunup, sunset ... grass with dew;
The birds singing ... tree frogs, too.
Why would one reject all this?
And bad health, run such a risk!
Nerves all tied in knots as string;
Close to nature ... no such thing.
Barefoot he walks, as he sings;
As he strolls, his catch he swings.
A happy boy ... so was he ...
A happier man, there cannot be!

Barefoot man ... still barefoot boy,
Still woods and streams are his joy;
Every tree, he knows by name ...
Growing up, he made a game –
Been awhile since he's been out,
To walk barefoot ... all about.
All things he liked ... proved the same;
And proved they did, with no blame.
He found he's the same inside ...
The little boy ... never died!
Little boy ... in body grown –
Loves to hunt and fish alone.
With nature, he is at ease ...
Barefoot, walking in the breeze;
Thinking how good his Lord is ...
Blessings given ... that are his –
As he ponders ... on his way...
Why should one ... because he's grown;
Think to live ... by rules alone.
Knowing there's a Judgment Day,
Accepting Christ ... when a boy ...
His life has been, filled with joy;
Six days barefoot ... he can roam;
Church on Sunday ... shoes he dons!

Continued

On way home from Church he thinks;
On Scriptures ... the preacher links.
Train a child, as he should go ...
He'll not depart ... then when old;
Knowing this is very true —,
Much to parents ... this is due;
A child molded, as is clay,
Always teaching ... truth, the way.
Since God made Heaven and earth,
Made the way of the New Birth ...
Through Jesus Christ, His own Son;
Nothing good that man has done.
When you look around and see,
All God's given us for free ...
God took care when we were small;
Everyone, by name, He calls.
Why should man turn from Him now?
In reverence ... we all should bow.
God owns the whole universe ...
Adam and Eve brought sin's curse.
God made man with power of choice;
Man has his say ... given voice.
Barefoot boy did love the Lord ...
Could barefoot man ... less afford!!!

Arkansas

(Triolet)

Arkansas is a beautiful state!
Abundant blessings, from God stream;
Scale to fifty ... a fifty does rate;
Arkansas is a beautiful state!
Four seasons: you choose a best of all;
Mountains, lakes, streams, with hills so green,
Arkansas is a beautiful state!
Abundant blessings, from God stream.

Sandman

Sleepy?
Go on to bed!
Nights are meant for sleeping;
For today much work is wed, so ...
To bed!

Triad

These three:
Faith, hope, charity,
Are the gifts that are left;
Greatest of these is charity, not ...
For self!

More Work!

Spinning!
In all patterns,
The spider spins its web,
Working its way into castles ...
No web!

Busy

The ant,
Keeps so busy,
Though has no boss;
No one tells it want to do, so ...
No break!

So Wise

Be wise,
Choose Christ, the Rock;
The Coney, though feeble
Makes its home in the hills and rocks;
Your choice!

The Zebra

All stripes!!
Exact in pattern;
You see nothing but stripes;
Black and white or white and black, even
On ears!

So Thankful He Cares

Trusting a loved one, who's far away:
Into a great God's loving care ...
Who knows everything ... night and day;
Our every thought to Him laid bare.

Our heart can be at peace in this;
After supplication made by prayer:
Faith needs press forward ... doubts resist;
By the devil, ... inspired not rare.

We must pray with faith believing;
That God does hear and answer prayer:
Only through faith ... all else leaving;
God can overrule, what others dare.

God limits the devil in his power;
He only has what God allows ...
God is the one, man answers to;
The one to whom ALL knees will bow.

If God be for us ... we can't fail;
In faith and trust with Him, proceed,
He's in charge ... to every detail;
Evil is subject to God ... decreed.

God can halt evil at His will;
He has the whole world in His hands:
Can quiet the storm with "Peace be still;"
His power reaches faraway lands.

Time Does Tell

(Villanelle)

We met long ago:
Near the village by the stream;
True love does last, through many woes.

It seems time ... so fast does go:
None gained by any means;
We met long ago.

God has blessed us so:
So much more than needs:
True love does last, through many woes.

Christ ... salvation for the soul,
Many years he has preached:
We met long ago.

Our four children still come home;
We right to them did teach ...
True love does last, through many woes.

Together ... older, we grow:
Heaven does closer gleam;
We met long ago:
True love does last, through many woes.

For: Carl

An Even Place

Our feet walk in an even place;
When we walk in God's truth ...
We reap benefits from God's grace;
When old or in our youth.

When feet stand in an even place;
One isn't prone to slide ...
In TRUTH ... running the Christian race;
For truth, our Saviour died.

Walk on in truth ... never turn back;
Feet are on solid rock ...
With faith in Christ, nothing you'll lack;
An even place ... though mocked.

A Way of Life

A beautiful, happy child ... born on a Sunday morn.
As flowers in spring or sunshine after the rain,
Or as a rainbow appears after the storm;
A joyous demeanor ... mostly the same.
Beautiful and most special – true to form.
Life to her is fun – but not a game.
No matter the circumstance – happy or forlorn;
Much ever the same, for excuses are lame!

Lending a helping hand to others is her view.
With her hand in God's Hand, she takes her stand.
It sometimes seems there are only a few.
But, following Christ – life can be grand,
This kind of spirit ... as refreshing as the dew.
A person need draw a line in the sand,
Then there won't be so many mistakes to rue!
If all had the same values across the land!

Enjoying the blessings God is always giving;
That's as it should be – to be sure.
It makes for rejoicing and abundant living;
For mean spirits and sour dispositions, a sure cure.
Circumstances – not our values deciding!
What God allows, we can certainly endure.
Strength comes from knowing – God's love abiding;
Knowing we are His – stand for right and feel secure!

Responsibility

Only the children can escape;
Responsibility for long ...
Little by little, as they grow –
More ... as they become strong.

None can forever be children ...
   ... Perhaps ... only in mind —;
Then it is considered ... sickness;
For which no one would pine.

Being responsible is a privilege ...
One should be thankful for –
With God's help, cross life's every bridge;
Faith leading ... crossing more.

A life that's given in service ...
Must staunchly take its place –
Face up, to what life holds ... the gist;
With love, faith and God's grace.

A stigma ... to not take one's place;
To hide away from life ...
Be useful ... not just take up space;
Health ... means face up, to strife.

A purpose, in life all do need —;
Not wandering aimlessly ...
Something, to live for ... taking the lead;
Not for babies ... indeed!

Grow up, let children be little;
You've had your turn, in time ...
Adults should not their lives riddle;
Teach love and faith ... combined.

Triolets

When he returned, he brought me a ring.
It was beautiful with my birthstone.
He said he loved me; my heart took wing!
When he returned he brought me a ring.
Cupid got two hearts with bow and string.
Two hearts loved, not one alone.
When he returned he brought me a ring.
It was beautiful, with my birthstone.

When we were moving to the West Coast,
My love met me on the way.
He drove out from the army post.
When we were moving to the West Coast,
Time was so short, could have seen a ghost!
Though summertime, a melancholy day.
When we were moving to the West Coast,
My love met me on the way.

His garden of tulips is beautiful!
Where a rainbow of colors combine.
Such a multitude, with nothing dull,
His garden of tulips is beautiful!
All who see, proclaim the beauty, dutiful,
As a variety of colors in garden you find,
His garden of tulips is beautiful!
Where a rainbow of colors combine.

He loves all kinds of roses,
Planting when he can!
Always ready with fertilizer and hoses,
He loves all kinds of roses,
Though, only some wake up noses,
He still works and tills the land.
He loves all kinds of roses,
Planting when he can!

Triolets

My little Shadow is a Schipperke,
She's a beautiful dog and intelligent,
She's the best of friends to me.
My little Shadow is a Schipperke,
Tries to protect me from all she sees.
No misunderstanding what is meant!
My little Shadow is a Schipperke,
She's a beautiful dog and intelligent.

So many things I love to do!
To read, write, paint and cook,
Those named are just a few!
So many things I love to do!
Always like learning something new!
At the beauty of nature I love to look,
So many things I love to do!
To read, write, paint and cook.

I have accepted Christ as my Savior,
Do you know Him in the free pardon of sin?
By conviction, the Holy Sprit draws you and me,
I have accepted Christ as my Savior,
Happiness fills the hearts of those who believe.
By grace through faith in Christ, Salvation depends!
I have accepted Christ as my Savior,
Do you know Him in the free pardon of sin?

Love should rule the home!
Each caring for the other,
When hearts are there, no need to roam,
Love should rule the home!
Selfishness one should not condone,
When young or with old age totter,
Love should rule the home!
Each caring for the other.

A Black Umbrella

Depression covers as a black umbrella ...
Always a dark shadow between you and the sun;
Blotting out light in the pit the devil dug,
With doubts hiding the face of God's only Son.

The devil's busy digging depression's pit;
Discouraging God's people ... so they won't look up
Toward Heaven – where God does sit on His throne,
Inviting our call, waiting with us to sup.

God created the world in all its beauty,
Giving man dominion to rule o'er the earth;
In beauty, man can dwell, and Salvation's free:
God's love and grace manifest in the New Birth.

Without faith, it's impossible to please God:
Faith removes the umbrella of despair ...
Depression's not of God! Oh, man of the sod!
But, the devil's best worn tool, and used to snare.

To please God, we walk by faith and not by sight:
Trust not thine own strength, but, faith with weakness mesh;
Faith lifts from depression's "pit" into God's light,
Where Christ, "The Light of the World," our hearts refresh.

Depression's Dark Umbrella

Discouragement is depression's deep pit,
With its own covering of deep despair;
If not stopped, one sinks deeper, bit by bit,
The dark umbrella is hard to bear ...
With sadness and despondency, cast down,
Head bowed, eyes averted, spirit so low;
Smile never graces the mouth, only a frown,
Depressed ones, it seems, are their own worst foe.
One step at a time, day by day, even less;
Must keep busy, doing something each day,
Looking to the Lord in faith, will give rest;
With much prayer and reading God's word each day;
Repentance of sin, will turn things about,
With faith versus doubt, depression can't mount!

Matters Not, Little or Grown!
(Terza Rima)

Vacation for some means work for others,
To have everything ready when they come;
Many extra things you try to get done ...

So there'll be time for all to have some fun;
So, you'll cook ahead what dishes you can ...
Then you can slow down, not be in a run;

Remembering the favorites ... you make again!
Family has grown, and to forget ... you're prone;
That little boy has grown into a man!

You've grown older, some, but you're not alone;
A few days isn't long for a visit ...
But, better than just talking on the phone;

From traveling so far, they're so worn and tired:
Those preparing seem never to get through;
Doing all things themselves, nothing to be hired.

Those coming are worn ... children grow tired, too:
Both traveler and host are not at their best ...
Visit! Forget the rest ... is what you need do!

Continued

Remember, they're family ... not just a guest;
The few days managed will be gone once more!
Time to get what enjoyment, you can wrest.

What things are done; don't let it be a chore;
Though tired ... they arrive with eyes shining brightly!
Advice ... enjoy what's good ... the rest ignore!

You must have done a few things that are right:
Them wanting to spend time at their old home ...
They just let things go ... planning how they might.

They're our children, it matters not, how old;
The news they bring ... always, varied and vast ...
Their visit is made possible by the Lord.

Blessings will be told and those of the past,
Causing faith to be increased ... doubts to fold;
Reminded ... burdens, on the Lord to cast.

Though tired and worn, much love each heart does hold;
All good things come from God ... family is one!

Coming or Going!

What goes around comes around!
As history repeats itself ...
Nothing new under the sun;
Circling, leaving where it left.

What goes around comes around!
Is something we all have heard;
Has to be when nothing's new –
Under the sun ... it's God's Word.

What comes around goes around!
At times, it begins to spin ...
What's the end may seem the start!
Coming from where it has been.

What comes around goes around!
And passing itself in time;
Everything seems a circle ...
Coming and going combined!

Continued

What goes around comes around!
Be watchful for the ending ...
If it be the beginning's end;
Or the end of the beginning!

As what goes, comes back around;
And what comes, goes on past!
"Nothing new," so old must be!
Yet, the time element ... vast!

What goes around comes around!
It's sometimes hard to tell which;
Spinning, casting a shadow ...
Turns as a merry-go-round!

What goes around comes around!
As history repeats itself ...
Nothing new under the sun –
Circling, hovering where it left.

Standing Appointment
(Limerick)

It's appointed to man once to die;
And after this is the judgment:
No push for head of line,
At either judgment time;
No one overlooked ... no passers by.

The Wimp
(Limerick)

A man did much to appease his wife,
Let go ALL important things in life;
While counting the cost,
Of what he had lost ...
She dreamed of being a rich man's wife.

Fragile?
(Limerick)

"Till death do us part," is what was said,
Those words were spoken when they were wed;
Vows were love's token,
 ... Soon to be broken:
But, by divorce ... not when they were dead.

The Inevitable
(Limerick)

Death stalks life, waits at every heart's door;
Never enough ... always seeking more:
Can't hide from it long ...
Living right or wrong;
Will catch you when old, IF not before!

Calories Can't Keep a Secret
(Quatrain)

When eating, no use in trying to hide,
Everyone will know ... no need to confide!
What's eaten in, "secret" will soon be seen;
As fat covers body ... that once was lean.

Why is it many people seem to think –
That "hidden eating," to lean bodies link;
Many foods ignored, when there's one to see,
When same food in " secret," eaten with glee.

What's eaten is never hidden for long ...
Though might be skipped many a dinner's gong!
That eaten excessively turns to fat;
Turned around ... like canary swallowed cat!

Served a salad at table ... calories few:
Those calories in "secret," will add up, too!
Rolls, biscuits, butter in "secret," not barred!
Against double candy bars, one must guard.

Takes more than pushing "away from table,"
The counting of calories must be stable –
It's into how many calories you dip ...
Always, seen on the hips ... what's passed the lips!

"Doctor, Doctor, Come Quick! Take a Closer Look"

Read fine print ... he or she may be a "quack," and not a doctor sent.
General practitioner is where we need to look ...
Specialists just do certain things to toe, neck or stint,
Either right or left hand, or overlapped tooth ... by the book.

No doubt going by the book ... they
Take time to give you a look ... Medicare on hook ...
Many have no heart for practice they are in,
Some take off "right" foot ... when "left" it should have been.

If your right hand is hurt, better check it twice ...
You may end up left-handed ...
Not like a Christmas list you can check on thrice!
You may feel "like stranded."

You may pay price not looking again ...
Just don't take an ... anesthesia ... the best way.
Just end the way you began ...
Grit your teeth and bear the pain;

Be tough, "Civil War days" limbs like cordwood are not few;
You can see what specialists cannot do;
Just do the best they can in lieu;
Courageous men ... not new.

Doctor no doubt will be in a huff
And his "efficient" nurse will, too ...
For then she can wipe up spilled
"Folie" from floor, and throw it upon you!

All doctors are not the same ...
  'Tis true ... some are very good, but
Better watch closely if you see a sign ... it may just be a game,
He only works on one side ... that will never do!

There may be missing tools
They may blame it on you ...
No doubt they can be found on an old stool;
Not on table or case or book of rules.

No deduction for Medicare they take for fraud ...
Just another order they pursue.
Put your left foot in, your right foot out.
"Ennie," "Minnie ..." which to do?

Medicare is going broke no doubt;
With all the fraud and "hullabaloo,"
As Medicare fraud does mount
Doctors to patients aren't being true.

You go for heart surgery, but doctor removes foot,
Not even the right one then ...
Can't tell which with all the soot.
If they'd only read book ... get on knees to God and pray ...

Review Hippocratic oath they should have
Known before graduation day.
When you get your bill and go pale,
Just remember ... the money trail!!

Ode on Money

Love of money's the root of all evil:
An all-knowing God admonishes us ...
Every sin reaching back from Adam's fall;
        Knows money's lust.

Coveting, pierces through with many sorrows:
Righteousness, godliness, faith, patience, love
Meekness, show the good profession witnessed;
        Here and above.

Medium of exchange ... pray, love not too well!
Life consisteth not in the things possessed;
The devil deceives: be wise as serpents ...
        Harmless as doves.

No man can serve two masters; he will hate
One and love the other, ye cannot serve
God and mammon! You choose, it isn't fate!
        Your choice is free.

God cares for the lilies of the field ... feeds
The fowl of the air; knows every sparrow
That falls: man's valued more, though sinful seed,
        Man has a soul.

Christ died for all ... He'll save all who believe:
We're born in sin; natural instincts, the same;
Envy is cruel, greed blinds and deceives ...
        Christ breaks sin's chain.

On the Money Trail
(Tercet)

Follow the money trail is frequently heard:
In public discourse and political news,
Corruption traced when secrecy's preferred.

All avenues are unscrupulously used;
Money's the cause of much upheaval,
Moneys' power is universally abused.

Love of money's the root of all evil:
The Bible, God's word, tells us this is so!
The same now, as back in times medieval.

The love of it will turn friend into foe:
Disregarding means ... he who would be rich,
Pierces himself through with many sorrows.

Money trail has more exits than access:
An underground maze like gopher or mole;
Many pitfalls, boulders and ravines,

For the dollar, many would sell their soul:
Lives wasted, looking back, when it's too late;
Scent of money on trail, makes many bold.

Riches make themselves wings and fly away,
As an eagle toward Heaven ... won't wait:
Men praise thee when thou doeth well to thyself.

Money trail, with happiness, keeps no date;
God's truth will never change ... or powers abate!

Trying, You May Succeed!
(Cinquain)

Old start ...
With someone new?
Or, new start with old mate;
That may save a marriage, home and
Divorce!

Who First?
(Cinquain)

Order
Of things should be:
God first, others second,
Yourself last and not ... the other
Way 'round.

Together
(Cinquain)

All for
One ... one for all;
A family ought to be:
Support, encourage, correct, chasten
With love.

Repeat!
(Cinquain)

What goes ...
'Round comes around;
A circle has no end,
Never stops when ... it begins to
Go 'round.

It Took a Child

Remember the tale of the Emperor,
Parading midst people wearing no clothes;
They were afraid to say he was naked ...
All but one, a child ... played dumb, kept their mouths closed.

The rest told him just how well he was dressed ...
Were politically blind to what was right;
Not a stitch of clothing! But none would confess;
What they ignored certainly wasn't trite.

There's a good lesson in this tale that was told ...
Now the question ... do people do the same?
There are some who stand for right and are bold;
Others pretend they don't know ... it's all a game.

What is wrong, that people just will not see:
Scandal in the Nation's Capitol plain,
Many like the Emperor's subjects be ...
Just shut their eyes to political bane.

The Emperor was deranged ... lost his mind;
And all the people were they crazy, too?
They pretended, collectively ... combined!
A child said he was naked, spoke what was true!

The Lord sees everything, just as it is:
Our every deed ... is mirrored back to Him;
It's as if we ALL live in a house of glass,
With every work and action taped on film.

What If!
(Triolet)

If criminals could decide their own fate,
Jails would stand empty, with criminals free!
Crime would increase sooner ... rather than late,
If criminals could decide their own fate,
There's be no judge or jury to debate ...
What punishment or sentence there would be;
If criminals could decide their own fate,
Jails would stand empty with criminals free!

Oh Me! Oh My!
(Triolet)

Oh me! Oh my! What a bumbling mess!
White House admits to so many "bumbles:"
Always finding MORE material than LESS!
Oh me! Oh my! What a bumbling mess!
"Crazy like a fox" ... faulty memories attest!
O'er files, tapes and records ... they ALL stumble;
Oh me! Oh my! What a bumbling mess!
White House admits to so many "bumbles!"

The Oyster
(Triolet)

The oyster, irritated by a grain of sand;
Goes to work in his confined space!
Run away! ... But he never can ...
The oyster, irritated by a grain of sand;
He'll work for relief ... and take his stand;
He'll make a pearl, with sand the base!
The oyster, irritated by a grain of sand;
Goes to work in his confined space!

Slick Politicians

So many times, as in politics we see;
How easy to tie themselves – chain and no key.
By weaving a web of lies – election time they pay a fee.
Slick enough like Houdini to escape, or seem to be;
Truth never leaves anyone – even a politician up a tree.
How we vote – God sees all – reckoning for you and me.
Our voting is not separated from our values.

Like Feathers
(Triolet)

Everyone has heard the old adage ...
That "birds" of a feather flock together;
Commonly known, yet, wisdom of a sage!
Everyone has heard the old adage ...
Just wait ... other, "birds" appear on stage;
Rushing to aid ... good sense won't deter ...
Everyone has heard the old adage ...
That "birds" of a feather flock together.

Guilty, Also!
(Triolet)
(2 John, Verse 11)

If to evil we bid God's speed,
The Bible says we're guilty, too;
And partakers of evil deeds ...
If to evil we bid God's speed,
And to God's word we don't give heed;
We're held accountable ... it's true;
If to evil we bid God's speed,
The Bible says we're guilty, too.

Flying High

Up in the sky, near moon and stars,
When there's trouble, there's scheduled plans;
Astronauts float around in space ...
Hooked to lines while working with hands.

The world has beauty ... its whole girth,
Yet, forsaken are God's rulings:
So many killings here on earth.
Abortions and drive-by shootings.

If "space" helps one getting to work,
Why not a "space station" for Congress?
Without "pork" and no voting perks ...
There's no incentive for largess.

The "White House" could be a "white capsule,"
Traveling ... turning ever so fast ...
Pundits might "spin" this ... a " legacy;"
And Air Force One's flying so vast!

A "bird's-eye" view by satellite seen,
Air Force One ... no longer needed.
Just like Jack and the stalk of bean,
What a "legacy" ... to him deeded.

Comeuppance

(From Proverbs 16)

Whoso rewardeth evil for good,
Evil shall not depart from his house:
Though trying to hide ... as if he could!

Majority of time, is saved to grouse;
An evil man will seek rebellion ...
A cruel messenger shall be sent to him.

He that justifieth the wicked ...
And he that condemneth the just, both
Are abomination to the Lord.

Silver and gold require refining pot,
And furnace: the Lord trieth the hearts,
Condemning ALL evil ... the heart – hides not!

A wicked doer gives heed to false lips,
And a liar giveth ear to a naughty tongue,
Heart o'erflows evil ... as honeycomb drips.

Instead of right ... the devil's brew sips;
Later can be seen, what sin hath wrought.

Cart Before the Horse

Animals gather food for winter;
Work to lay by ... in store ...
Birds build nests ... let nothing hinder;
Eggs laid then ... not before.

Seems we humans would do better;
Following their decree ...
Often we become a debtor ...
Plan for naught ... take no heed.

Man can work, think and make his plans;
Yet, many never do ...
With negligence and idle hands;
Fails a home to pursue.

Married ... children start to arrive;
With no place yet to go ...
Best to work, plan, and take some pride;
Trust God's help ... "hoe your row."

Animals know to build their home;
Bird's instinct says, ... "Build nest ..."
No one to prod ... they're on their own;
House comes first ... then the rest.

Man seems prone to do things backwards;
Put cart before the horse ...
Should use sense ... as animals and birds;
HOUSE ... with no need of force.

Senryu

Pawnshop ...
Wedding bands ... all sizes sold for
Toe rings.

Senryu

The twig ...
With care, won't be recognized
When a tree.

From Hand to Foot
(Cinquain)

A ring ...
For bride or groom
Cherished at the wedding
Fill pawnshop showcases ... sold for
Toe rings.

Smiling
(Triolet)

They say smiling burns sixty-five calories;
If this is true ... there's many sad people!
Many overweight ... everyone agrees!
They say smiling burns sixty-five calories;
You've never seen a " fat" laughing hyena!
Remember this! Let your laugh be liberal;
They say smiling burns sixty-five calories
If this is true ... there's many sad people!

Senryu

A horse
Of a different color could
Be the same one

Sneryu

Let another
Praise you ... then it
Isn't boasting

Senryu

Don't tell ...
Just show by what
You do

Senryu

Money earned...
Usually outlasts an inheritance
Easily obtained

Senryu

Money worked for ...
Stretches further than a gift
Unexpected

Haiku

The wind ...
Blowing in the trees
Looks cool!

Haiku

Dark moon ...
Stars up so high
Black night

Senryu

Cold outside ...
Heavy, warm jacket
Legs bare!

Senryu

A baby!
Then mother goes to work ...
Somewheres else!

Now ... Don't Forget!
(Cinquain)

Thank you ...
Don't forget to
Say! ...You need learn while small
It's good manners ... you can discard
When grown.

Haiku

Spring rains ...
The air is so clean
Much mud!

Test Day!
(Cinquain)

Some come early
Others just make it on
Time ... trying to keep eyes open
For sight.

Haiku

Eyes bright ...
Laughing inside
Joke on self

Haiku

No smile ...
Eyes dancing light
Secret known

Haiku

Rosebush ...
Perfume in trees
No hybrid

Haiku

Cool breeze!
Sunset behind mountain!
Hammock!

Haiku

So quiet …
Eyes a sparkle
Can't deceive!

Haiku

Tall tales …
Eyes do resist
To tell

Haiku

Black out …
Actions with words
Remain blurred

Haiku

Cancel …
Words with actions!
Progress

Haiku

Lazy ...
A beachcomber
No hurry

Haiku

Deep snow ...
Molds garden of shrubs
To fantasy

Haiku

Not hungry ...
Will eat anything
A ruse

Haiku

Snowfall ...
Sculptured beauty
Pristine

Haiku

Sunshine ...
Blue water of lake,
The sky!

Haiku

Acorn falls ...
Time, sunshine and rain:
An oak

Haiku

Quiet zone ...
Solitude on the lake
Fish in school

Haiku

Tiny ant ...
Works without a break
No coffee!

Haiku

Night sky
A million points of light
Star gaze

Haiku

Gold watch
Given at retirement
Sleep in!

Move On
(Cinquain)

The lake ...
With the lily
Pads, is a frog's playground,
Until the fisherman casts with
Delight.

Two Ways
(Cinquain)

Man's way ...
Do to others
Before they do to you!
God's way: Do, as you'd have them do
To you.

All Mine!
(Cinquain)

That's mine!
And I'll keep it.
What's yours will be mine if
I can get it; then it all will
Be mine.

Haiku

Hands sweep ...
Time on past
What's now?

Haiku

Good news ...
Always too short –
Bad news

Haiku

The canopy ...
Clouds or clear
In place

Haiku

Bermuda Triangle ...
On sock always missing
To every pair

Haiku

The rose ...
In beauty picked
Pressed in book

Before Not After

Do we show our love for others ...
As we should ... while we can –
Father, mother, sisters, brothers;
Not always be on hand.

After one's left this life of strife;
Their life to others means much more –
In death ... departing of this life;
There's many to adore.

Why not take time to let them know;
True feelings of your heart ...
Express your love – then let it show;
Actions play such a part.

Prayer, kind words of encouragement;
Will help in troubled times ...
Just knowing your support, they're lent;
Withholding ... such a crime.

Flowers for the dead ... who won't know;
Give them something for NOW ...
To enjoy ... their thankfulness show;
Shortcomings ... do ... allow!

What's in A Name?

So many names ... some short – some long – some
    liked ... many not;
In olden times much significance was placed in
    a name given to we of the sod;
A name had meaning – bearing the responsibility
    of it – became your lot.
So important – Jesus our Savior, and John the Baptist ...
    names were announced by the angel, Gabriel, a messenger
    sent from God.

When people acquainted with us hear our name – what
    immediately comes to mind ... ?
Are the values we profess – made manifest that we possess,
    in the way we live our life—?
In years gone by – it was said – "A person was only as
    good as their word"— a time to remind!!
A handshake – a "gentleman's agreement" – binding both
    parties – a deal consummated – the ending of strife.

A name is of importance – yet more the values of the one –
    on whom the name is bestowed.
Christian virtues should be desired to be paramount – not
    just a name of renown;
Proverbs 22:1 – "A good name is rather to be chosen than
    great riches – and loving favor rather than silver and gold."
A statement easily understood by all – and so explicitly
    profound.

Variety

Children are so much fun ... while small;
Four will keep you busy ...
Many memories we can recall —;
Jumbled ... can grow dizzy.

So different ... yet, fun with all four;
If children keep you young –
The playing then ... would now make sore;
Aches and pains ... aging has done.

All liked music ... they loved to sing;
Their lessons did begin ...
Each, with the piano had their fling;
For some ... was ball ... to win.

One daughter ... liked better to sing;
The other ... piano ... played —;
Practice bell ... boys ignored its ring;
With ball and bat ... they stayed.

Four can put you through the paces;
Exhausting to keep ... up ...
Happiness shining on their faces –
Growing up ... can disrupt.

Spirit Renewed
(2 Cor. 4:16)

While the outward man is perishing,
The inward man's renewed day by day:
Although saved ... more signs of aging seen,
Only death will hold old age at bay.

Growing feeble and steps uncertain ...
Eyes dim ... wrinkles line the parchment face,
Strength fails; small things become such burdens;
Thinking what might have been, without grace.

Youth's energy abounded for years ...
The years moved swiftly, for time passed fast;
Much slowed down, for to age, days are geared,
Aches and pains can into doldrums cast.

A body once strong, now, just creeps along,
Weakness overcomes where strength has been;
Dull ears fail to hear even bird's song ...
'Twas Adam's fall ... plunged all into sin.

Continued

Through Christ, the inward man's made alive,
God's Great Salvation brings peace sublime;
When it's time to cross the Great Divide,
The inward man renewed ... cannot die!

In Heaven, there'll be none of sin's wage,
All will be contentment, peace and joy ...
In Hell, lost souls spend ... eternal age;
With Christ, there'll be no sin to annoy.

Aging comes because of Adam's sin ...
Aches and pains, part of aging process,
Heaven's so different to what has been;
Living with Jesus freed from life's stress.

In Ecclesiastes, the twelfth chapter,
We read the allegory on old age ...
All this refers to the outward man:
The inward man's renewed day by day!

Real Love

I'm saved!
Salvation's free!
Christ died to save the lost;
He shed His blood on Calvary's tree,
For me.

When God Forgets
(Hosea 4:6)

In times past, God has destroyed His people,
For lack of knowledge ... God rejected them;
Since thou hast forgotten the law of God ...
God told them He would forget their children.

Children are a heritage of the Lord ...
They're not ours; they're only on loan from God:
Training children right is His just reward;
Bible teaching of discipline ... not mod!

We're to train a child in the way he should go,
When he's old he will not depart from it;
Loving parents to sinful things say, "no"...
Teaching them Christ died their sin to remit.

Enough wrong is done without encouragement;
A sad day when abortion was legalized ...
What a message to young people was sent!
Condoning sanctity of life's demise.

We go to war over "ethnic cleansing ..."
And with the shattering of bombs, kill the more,
Partial birth abortion is inhumane!
God's the giver of life ... judgment's in store.

Prayer was taken out of the public school ...
When tragedy strikes, they return to prayer;
"There is no God ..." the assumption of the fool,
Are there those who stand for Christ? Who will dare?

God forgets because of parents ...
Neglecting their duty to teach right,
Killings, drugs, violence attest to the fact;
The value of life in decline ... made trite.

If we would have God remember our children,
Parents must not forget the law of God ...
As we learn, we teach, living before them;
Not winking at sin or ... giving the nod.

The Lord tells us to draw nigh unto Him ...
When we do this, He'll draw nigh unto us;
Adult footprints for right ... grow ever dim,
They're obscured by greed, lack of faith and trust.

Another Year???

Another year it'll be for some,
For some, another day won't come;
Time allotted is in God's hand ...
Either long life or one just began.

New Year's resolutions pile up,
Unused ... to overflow life's cup;
Seldom used and forgotten ones,
Make a long, long list ... the total sum.

Inside the heart's the place to start,
Where seat of man's affection is ...
Only Christ can make the heart new;
And evil ways desired, eschew.

God's Word, the basis for what's right,
Jesus came to give the world light;
God gave His Son ... Saviour of man,
To redeem man's soul ... only HE can.

Salvation isn't ... by the year ...
It's ETERNAL and grows more dear;
Resolutions ... you think to make,
Without the "HEART" ... will a wrong turn take.

It's a decision to accept Christ,
Not resolutions that change a heart:
Another Year??? No one can tell!
When time's up ... it's Heaven or Hell.

My Family and I
(Written in 1966)

My family is just quite a mess!
The biggest to the least are full of jest.
So much going on at times it seems;
It's almost as if we had two teams.

Laughter is good for mind and heart,
But, sometimes seems we've got a head start.
Then again over trivial things,
Such an upset and grievous pains!

We worry and fret, instead of pray,
Therefore, the consequences, we must pay.
Seeing things in wrong perspective,
Causes so much grief and is deceptive.

Continued

Then, something comes, which needs much strength,
We all go on our knees at length,
And ask our Lord to hold us up,
To hear our prayers, and with us sup.

We never appreciate being together,
As much as our hearts tell us, when we're scattered.
One always knows, the others pray,
For being together, soon one day.

Then, like always, we take for granted ...
The times we long for when we're parted.
As we grow together in grace,
Looking back should increase our faith.

Knowing our Lord is ever faithful,
Our lives should not be barren, but fruitful.
What matters how far apart in miles?
We know we can be near each other ... and to God.

My Prayer
(Written in 1959)

Lord, increase my faith, I pray,
May I grow stronger in Thy grace,
Help me be submissive to Thy Will, each day,
And run with patience the Christian race.

Help me be ready to do Thy Will,
No matter how great or small it may seem,
May I go forward and never shirk,
But, labor abundantly, lost time to redeem.

Lord, help me to show how thankful I am,
For blessings Thou givest each day,
May my life point sinners to Calvary's Lamb,
And not hinder those who struggle along life's way.

Lord, help me to stand firm whatever the cost,
For the doctrines laid down in Thy Holy Word.
May I never compromise even to physical life lost,
But, always with Thy truth be gird.

Although there be things I can't understand,
When trials and troubles come;
I would not hearken to the voice of man,
But, may I, in humble submission say, "Lord, Thy Will be done."

My Savior Cares For Me
(Written in 1966)

I know my Saviour cares for me,
He proves it day by day,
He leads me, guides, directs my path,
As I journey along life's way.

I know my Saviour cares for me,
He is the Bishop of my soul,
He gives great peace down deep inside,
To last forever, while ages roll.

I know my Saviour cares for me,
He is always near to lighten my load,
When under life's burdens I become weary,
His Hands so strong help faltering feet
 along the narrow road.

I know My Saviour cares for me,
His every blessing, from love does stem,
He tries my faith through trouble and strife,
Do I prove that I love Him?

I know my Saviour cares for me,
May each day of life I live,
Show forth this love shed abroad, within,
And glory and honor to His Name give.

God's Love Never Fails

(Written in 1960)

In love, God sent His only Son,
To die on the Cross.
To save the souls of sinners;
That we need not be forever lost.

Christ's Love was made manifest,
He died that wretched death.
In Gethsemane, the battle won;
Prayed ... "Not my Will but Thine, be done."

Those who trust Christ need never fear,
Their Salvation is secure.
God in His Love gave this plan;
For the redemption of fallen man.

We are weak, earthy and frail,
But, our loving God loves us still.
God's Love abides and never fails.
God's Love so great, shall forever endure.

Believe the Lord
(Written in 1960)

Believe the Lord in all His promises,
His Word is true; He'll see you through
    every trial and misfortune.
Never falter in the way where the Lord is leading.
Though rough the road, with many thorns to pierce you,
Christ, our Lord, is the Companion who stays close to your side;
He protects, lest the thorns prick too deeply.
Troubles only draw us nearer His side so He can comfort;
And we will desire in His Will to abide.
His Love is shown in many ways, if we only take
    time to meditate upon the blessings He gives everyday.
We don't deserve His matchless Love,
Only God's grace sent Christ from Above to die the terrible
    death He died. –
To save my soul, He was crucified.
All He asks is that I believe for Salvation that will last for Eternity.
I believe my Lord on High.
Give me grace to live for Thee while here on earth,
And may if needed die for Thee in love, as Thou didst die for me.
Let my life mean no more to me than Thine to Thee,
When you gave it on Calvary to save my soul
    and set me free.
    I believe.

Storm Clouds of Life
(Written in 1960)

When storm clouds gather, and darken the sky;
The thunder rolls heavily and the wind is high;
We are made to rejoice when the sun shines through,
There is peace and calm, and the sky is again blue.
When storm clouds hover o'er life's pathway;
When sore the trials and troubles, and sever the test;
With the eye of faith, we can see light break through,
When to others it seems, we have lost in the battle for right.
There's One nearby to sustain and guide,
With nail-scarred hands pointing onward and upward;
Victory is ours ... the battle is won; if we only in His Will abide.
He is faithful and always at our side.

Lord, Help Me

(Written in 1966)

Lord, I pray Thee, help me,
To tell what's in my heart;
To those around about me,
Who are walking in the dark.

Lord, may I not falter, ever,
To witness as I can;
To those who need Thy comfort,
May I lend a helping hand.

Lord, I would draw closer to Thee,
To have the strength I need;
To help some poor lost sinner,
And in the right way lead.

Lord, help my faith grow stronger,
In spite of all adversity;
That I might help a child of Thine,
To heavily on Thee lean.

Lord, help me know my weakness,
The stronger in body I seem;
That you may receive all Glory,
For all things good are from Thee.

Lord, help me to always be thankful,
For loved ones, dear friends and all;
Who in the time most needed,
Were there without ever a call.

Lord, help me to always be thankful,
For prayers and all kindnesses shown;
For every token of love for me,
And for my dear loved ones at home.

For all these things ... I thank Thee.

Life
(Written in 1966)

Life without the Lord is empty,
Dreary, futile ... 'tis as an empty shell,
And full of heartache, pain and sorrow,
For the wayward soul on his road to hell.

Life with Christ is full and fruitful,
If we but follow His Holy Word,
We have peace, contentment, pleasure,
As we strive to serve our Lord.

The Savior's Love
(Written in 1966)

May we who know the Savior's Love
Not hinder those who would seek His face Above,
But, let our lives so consecrated be
That poor sinners in a darkened world
A ray of light may see.
That our earthly deeds would always point,
The lost to Calvary.

The Love of Money
(Written in 1956)

The love of money is the root of all evil;
In God's word we are told.
For money, men lie, steal and kill,
What wouldn't man do for a dollar?

Pirates and robbers take that which belongs to others,
Cause children to go hungry and cold.
"This is a terrible crime," we cry,
"And should be punished for being so bold?"

ALAS! STOP! THINK. Christian soul!
What value do YOU place on a dollar?
Does love of it come first in life,
And lack of it cause torment and strife?

Do you neglect the work of God,
Do we lack Missionaries to preach the word?
Does worldly gain come first with you,
Or to rescue some soul from satan?

Is the church house run down?
Are the doors about to fall?
Are things left undone which should be done,
Because the offerings fall?

Is the preacher poorly paid?
Are the pews almost empty?
For there's no time to worship God,
Another dollar is in the making!

Do you work six days a week, and overtime if needed,
Always there to punch the clock and never late at all,
But, Sunday morning always late, IF you come at all,
It's queer that relaxation's needed on Sunday, worst of all.

When the collection plate is passed,
Do you really sacrifice?
Or does sacrifice mean to you,
Giving what is left after your spending is through?

Christ truly sacrificed His life for you,
Then will you use that term so loosely,
And describe the little you give?
We're still unprofitable servants after we've
  done all that's our duty to do.

If you are stingy in your offerings to God,
And instead of the widow's mite,
You give what you might have left,
Then don't ask why, when instead of blessings,
  God uses His chastening rod!

WAKE UP! Dear Christian Soul,
The love of money has taken its toll,
When we forget the house of God,
Then say, "Oh, Lord, I love Thee so!"

For thirty pieces of silver my Savior was sold,
The love of money made Judas bold.
How Christ was betrayed is a story of old.
Christian Soul, beware lest your influence
  to the devil is sold!

By withholding that which belongs to God,
You miss blessings, which would be yours.
If you but placed value where value belongs,
And putting GOD first, you can't go wrong!

Are You as Rich as I?
(Written in 1951)

A rich man while admiring his grand estate,
Was annoyed to see a beggar watching outside the gate.
He called to him to be on his way,
But, to his surprise he made this reply,
"Are you as rich as I?"

You are rich in this world's goods,
You have your land, your mansion and money,
And I, though poor and shabbily dressed,
Will someday dwell in mansion on high ...
"Are you s rich as I?"

You worry and fret over problems of wealth,
 Afraid of losing what you've gained,
While I know my treasure in secure,
For in skies, moth and rust doth not corrupt,
And thieves cannot enter in.
"Are you as rich as I?"

You are a nobleman of stately birth,
In which titles and names are temporal.
By Spiritual birth, I am joint–heirs with Jesus Christ,
A child of the Heavenly King.
"Are you as rich as I?"

You, too, can be at peace with God,
And happy all the while.
If you'll accept the Christ who died,
And let Him within your heart abide,
"You, too, can be as rich as I."

Dear Reader:

This is Maxine's last book of poetry. If you haven't yet read *Sand and Pearls*, *Voice of the Heart* or *Mither*, you're missing a blessing! We hope that *Poetic Potpourri* inspired your life and refreshed your spirit. Maxine said that her purpose in writing poetry was to "touch the human heart." If you would like to contact us, we may be reached at P.O. Box 82, Conway, Arkansas 72033

May you receive a blessing from these poems.